D1274597

The Innovative EXECUTIVE

The Innovat▮ve EXECUT▮VE

LEADING INTELLIGENTLY IN THE AGE OF DISRUPTION

BELLA RUSHI

FOREWORD BY MAGNUS PENKER

WALL STREET JOURNAL AND *USA TODAY* BESTSELLING AUTHOR

Forefront
BOOKS

The Innovative Executive
Leading Intelligently in the Age of Disruption

© 2022 Bella Rushi

Published by Forefront Books.
Cover Design by Bruce Gore, Gore Studio, Inc.
Interior Design by Mary Susan Oleson, Blu Design Concepts

ISBN: 978-1-63763-084-6 print
ISBN: 978-1-63763-085-3 e-Book

Library of Congress Control Number: 2022902235

To my parents and my amazing kids

My parents taught me to be adaptable and always kind,
and they helped me find the courage to
follow my heart—thank you.

Zara, Rahul, and Ravi—thank you for the love,
laughter, and support you have given me
each and every day.

CONTENTS

PART III
Making the Most of
Your Technology Spend

FOREWORD

THE INNOVATIVE EXECUTIVE is a highly practical handbook on how to succeed with market-driven innovation to create chain reactions across the board. In a rare personal way, Bella Rushi walks you step by step how to build a culture of innovation driving sustainable growth. Follow her from a childhood of working with her dad as a street vendor to becoming an international extern and top consultant in innovation.

With firsthand experience explained using well-known examples grounded in world-class methodology, Bella Rushi opens up the doors to understand what is really important and how to use those insights in a daily practical perspective. Get acquainted with marketing, communication, narrative, testing with hypotheses, and when to pull the plug or not. It is a pleasure to recommend this book to anyone who wants to understand more and get practical insights into innovation management. Get ready to generate chain reactions and take your organization to the top with Bella Rushi in *The Innovative Executive*.

Many business leaders will recognize themselves in the examples and will find themselves rooting for Bella to succeed in her work harnessing innovation to turn their companies around. This book provides not only insights but defines a proven framework as a conversation versus a set of rules to follow. *The Innovative Executive* presents an ongoing discussion between readers and the author of what new practices can be integrated with effective decision-making to become an innovative business leader.

Bella's book is not only based on her own experiences, but it's the perfect illustration of how one needs to be able to pivot on a moment's notice depending on what the day's events bring forth in business. She uses the street vendor analogy as an ongoing theme in the book to demonstrate in today's ever-changing marketplace that business leaders need to develop the sharp mindset of a street vendor.

Bella shows the connection between the entrepreneurship mindset and the importance of innovation. She showcases how companies grow, especially in difficult environments, and how that growth increases over time. Bella outlines various methods that contribute to collecting new customer insights, creating new market segments, and outlining ways to maximize customer engagement strategies.

The timing of *The Innovative Executive* is perfect. Many leaders will change the ways they conduct business over the next five years, and only a handful of companies are equipped to face the challenges ahead. Bella insightfully builds on the examples from her own experiences and opportunities to introduce the strong capabilities needed to capture new growth. She suggests that embedding innovation practices is key to long-term growth. She also makes a very strong case for making data-driven decisions with the customer top of mind. You'll learn new capabilities such as being more customer-centric, adapting your core focus to meet shifting customer needs, addressing new opportunities through collaboration, reevaluating your business model, and remaining competitive through sustainability initiatives. This book will help you solve seemingly impossible challenges around innovation-led growth and forgo playing it safe to take more urgent actions.

Magnus Penker is the author of *Play Bold: How to Win the Business Game Through Creative Destruction*. He is an Innovation Thought Leader, CEO of Innovation360 Group, and a speaker in prestigious global forums and events such as The Global Peter Drucker Forum.

AN INVITATION

The seduction of safety is always more brutal and more dangerous than the illusion of discomfort.

—Robin Sharma[1]

EVERY BUSINESS LEADER understands that innovation is vital to an organization's success—perhaps even to its survival. Life will always throw curveballs at you—the mass disruption of the COVID-19 pandemic serves as a stark reminder of this fact—and the ability to innovate is what separates those businesses that survive from those that do not.

So how can a leader foster the culture of innovation that will someday be needed to ensure the survival of their business?

The path to innovation is a mindset—a willingness to promote creativity and precision. It's a structured discipline that requires pilot testing, experimentation, and meticulous data collection. It requires a sense of purpose—a drive to reach your goals combined with a capacity to pivot toward new ones when necessary. This journey creates new learnings, new experiences, new bonds, and new products and services, and with each step on the journey you become more confident, more flexible, and more adaptable to uncertain environments. And that flexibility is what allows you to thrive.

This understanding is what has enabled many business leaders to guide their organization to a sustainable level of new success: Fuji Films, Apple, Nintendo, LEGO, Netflix, Starbucks, and Marvel, to name just a few.

Change is hard, not just in our organizations but also in environments. Many companies constantly operate in a reactive mode and struggle to accomplish their goals. The leaders of these organizations are bombarded by confusing market signals and trends such as disruptive political events, the pandemic, and relentlessly rapid advances in technology. They have little clarity about which direction they should take, and they're terrified of making wrong decisions. They're inundated with overwhelming amounts of data, and they can't tell which data should be trusted. Then when change happens, the organizational culture becomes resistant and doubtful. This leads to unproductive and siloed departments.

Handling a crisis is not a onetime effort; it requires experience, flexibility, adaptability, and strong capabilities in your organization to move forward.

The goal of this book is to fill the following gaps in your understanding:

- What do companies need from their leaders today?

- What can we do to uncover new possibilities to go to market and to create new processes and new customer experiences?

14

- What is the real challenge companies face when it comes to innovation?

This book looks at three levers that business leaders can use to spur innovation: their business model, technology, and collaboration with external parties. It discusses the individual effects of these levers on organizational processes to make them more adaptable. It also analyzes the strengths of specific combinations of organizational capabilities, including those that are technology oriented, internally oriented, externally oriented, and those that integrate all these levers.

Each chapter provides insights drawn from practical case studies in which companies have used their capabilities to gain customer insight, build market share, and create long-term growth. I argue that prioritizing innovation is an important discipline that a company can add to its existing processes, business model, and customer experience. I explore the principles and capabilities of innovation and show how it can be embedded into a structured approach to become more adaptable and grow your company in a variety of highly competitive environments.

Too often, business leaders lose their focus when they become preoccupied by forces such as fear, conflict, and anxiety. This makes them reactive to challenging situations and causes them to become overly rigid and closed to influence. This in turn can lead to alienation from the people whose counsel they depend on and can cause them to lose command of their own strengths and resources.

This book is about making you an effective leader who will learn to enable flexible thinking and adaptability. My goal is to reconnect you with an entrepreneurial mindset that will allow you to create social capital through innovation, encourage risk-taking, create network expansion, and promote team spirit.

That may sound like a pretty lofty goal, but I'm well qualified to achieve it. I have considerable experience working with midsize and Fortune 500 companies in the areas of innovation strategy consulting, brand planning, advertising agency, integrated marketing communications, supply chain management, and regulatory compliance. Many consultants have a background in one or perhaps two of these areas—I have consulted with Fortune 500 companies in *all* of them.

My journey started with a degree in microbiology, the pursuit of which taught me to approach any scientific inquiry using a diverse lens to examine information and to propose evidence-based explanations. These values are a thread that runs throughout my twenty years in life sciences and the consumer products industry conforming to regulatory policies and standards, optimizing supply chain management to meet customer expectations, and developing integrated marketing communications strategies that delight the customer. These learnings have carried over into my current work, which is focused on building innovation strategies for midsize and Fortune 500 companies and conducting organizational innovation assessments to improve the viability of these companies.

Looking back on my experiences, I can see that my learnings have connected three distinct passions: *exploration*, or continuing to seek new opportunities as a scientist through observations and interviews; *integration* using cross-disciplinary skills from science, business management, supply chain management, and marketing; and *data* to plan, examine, increase efficiencies, and develop capabilities to solve problems and connect with customers.

This connection between entrepreneurship and innovation will promote greater flexibility and adaptation in any of your business activities, which benefits society, industry, and, ultimately, your business.

I invite you to join me on this very exciting journey!

PART I
Rethinking Your Business Model

1

THINK LIKE
A STREET VENDOR

You Can't Control Everything,
but You Can Deal with Anything

ENTREPRENEURSHIP is not "natural"; it is not "creative." It is work. . . . Entrepreneurship and innovation can be achieved by any business. . . . They can be learned, but it requires effort. Entrepreneurial businesses treat Entrepreneurship as a duty. They are disciplined about it . . . they work at it . . . they practice it.

—PETER DRUCKER[1]

LIFE IS NOT A SMOOTH, frictionless glide from point A to point B; the unexpected will always happen, whether it is a financial crisis or some kind of environmental or political disaster. Most businesses understand that. The question is whether they are doing anything about it. When something unexpected does come up, are they prepared to handle it?

I'm an innovation strategy consultant but when I was a child I worked with my dad as a street vendor, selling newspapers on Roosevelt Boulevard in Philadelphia, and that experience taught me one thing above all else: if you want to survive in an uncertain world where anything can happen at any time, you need to be flexible and adaptable. External factors will always arise to complicate your plans and impede your progress, but if you're nimble and prepared, you can always cope.

THINK LIKE A STREET VENDOR: BE ADAPTABLE, FLEXIBLE, AND DRIVEN

When you look at street vendors, regardless of what they're selling—newspapers, hot dogs, pretzels, flowers, or whatever—what do they all have in common? Above all else, they are adaptable.

When I was one of those vendors, we all knew when we had to take our newspapers and run to the other side of the street because the heavier traffic was there. When there was a road closure, we knew that we might need to move a couple of blocks down and set up shop there instead of in our usual spots.

We would get out there by 7:00 in the morning, even on a

Saturday or Sunday, in order to catch the early risers. We knew how and when to respond to bad weather, bad road conditions, or whatever that day's challenge might be. On really hot days, we used to come with mini–water bottles to hand out for free with our newspapers—because they were cheap and helped us to sell more of our inventory.

The most important thing for a street vendor is to become so flexible that you're always thinking ahead of the customer. You're forced to think on your feet all the time about what the customer is feeling today and how to best serve them. Since street vendors are exposed to ever-changing and sometimes harsh conditions, they develop empathy and feel the need to alleviate others' pain by devising solutions.

So all street vendors have intuition and flexibility in common—but just as important, they have tremendous drive. In business, we call that *purpose*. Street vendors have to be driven because many of them won't earn enough to eat if they don't sell all of their hot dogs or water bottles or whatever it is they're selling. In order to provide food for their families, they must always be driven and flexible.

Seen in this light, street vendors are a great example of entrepreneurs who are always ready for the market, always thinking, *What can we do if things don't work out? How do I get rid of my inventory? How do I satisfy my customer?* Every day you learn something new. You adapt.

I have seen those same qualities and that same attention to ever-changing external factors in the companies that have survived the economic crisis brought on by the COVID-19 pandemic. When the pandemic first struck, they already had the strong drive they would need to get them through it—that same entrepreneurial drive they had when the company first launched, the reason they started the business in the first place. That drive motivates you to serve the customer and the community as opposed to a shortsighted desire for near-term profits. It is the voice within you that says, *I really want to get this product and this service out to the customer or the supplier or the vendor—so how am I going to do that?* The same drive that inspired you in the first place motivates you to start brainstorming: *What can I do?*

My family had three different newsstands, and my brother, my dad, and I would each work one of them. Our first priority was to make sure we didn't go home with any newspapers—that's drive number one. You don't want to be left with any inventory.

Many companies, both small and large, develop long-range business plans: they set up a plan for the current year and a plan for next year. The plan for the following year is flexible, but ironically the plans for current years are usually rigid. I have seen this firsthand, over and over, throughout my career as a consultant. They are not flexible at all. Many companies want predictability and control over the future. If external factors suddenly cause new problems to arise, how are they going to maneuver around them if they have a rigid plan?

You constantly have to adapt to new circumstances, just as my family and I had to adapt to whatever conditions existed on Roosevelt Boulevard on any given day: a car crashes or the road is closed in one section and an ambulance arrives, and now you are losing an hour and a half of sale time—what do you do?

A CEO doesn't have to have experience as a street vendor to understand this, but they do have to have that sense of urgency and necessity—that sense of drive.

START WITH YOUR PURPOSE

Founded in 1902, 3M (best known for its most famous invention, the Post-it note) has been a constant presence on the Fortune 500 list for the last hundred years. In that time, they have made sixty thousand products—a third of which were invented within the last five years.[2]

But even the most innovative company can be affected by unexpected external events, and like many other companies, 3M struggled during the pandemic—their sales slipped in a number of areas, including oral care, office supplies, industrial glues, and automotive manufacturing. The company had to furlough a number of its employees, and one-quarter of 3M's factories had closed by April 2020.

On the other hand, the company's sales grew 2.7 percent, to $8.08 billion,[3] in just the first quarter of 2020—a much better result than the Wall Street forecast of $7.91 billion. This was, of course, partly because 3M's N95 face masks and other personal protective equipment were suddenly in high demand.[4] Because they had strong portfolios in different markets, they were able to pivot their focus, increasing production for PPE such as masks, respirators, and ventilators and collaborating with other companies such as Ford to develop PPE. (We'll discuss the topic of collaboration at greater length in chapters 8 and 9.)

Because of the vastness of the company's portfolio, 3M products are found in many different industries. Creating so many new products (again, over sixty thousand of them!) and launching them to market successfully takes commitment and years of practice—and a culture with an innovative mindset. For over a century, 3M has demonstrated that mindset.

What else separates 3M from rivals such as United Technologies, DowDuPont, General Electric, and Arconic?[5]

- 3M has developed products that have cross-disciplinary capabilities so they can be made by the same methods and machines.

- They protect their patents and invest in R&D during good times and bad times (a critical practice and discipline much needed for all industries today).

- They focus on metrics that clearly define what constitutes a new product.

Just as important, in its early years 3M introduced a "15 percent rule"[6] that allowed employees to use 15 percent of their work time to pursue their own programs and product development ideas. This intentional direction and support from senior management is what allows 3M employees to explore and innovate, having a mindset of a street vendor to spark creativity.

3M succeeds because the company aligns everything it does with a higher purpose and a clear set of values—most especially a respect for science. The company's vision embraces technology to improve life through innovation, and its values also encompass diversity, inclusion, and sustainability (a set of topics we'll discuss at length in chapter 12). Like a street vendor, 3M has had to be flexible and adaptable in order to succeed. As retired 3M vice president of human resources Gordon Engdahl said, "3M has a tolerance for tinkerers and a pattern of experimentation that led to our broadly based, diversified company today. To borrow a line from *Finian's Rainbow*, you might say we learned to 'follow the fellow who follows a dream.'"[7]

Ultimately, whether you have the wherewithal to find solutions to your problems comes down to knowing your strengths and your internal capabilities. Those capabilities encompass everything from your supply chain to your customer insights to your operations to your understanding of what your value proposition is—and all of these things matter, so if they are not strong in the first place, then when external factors actually hit your industry, it will be difficult for you to pivot and adapt.

Of course, out-of-the-blue, "act of God" types of events are not the only kinds of unforeseen challenges you'll have to cope with. Even in more predictable "normal" times, change is a constant. As time passes, the public's needs and desires continuously change, and customer habits are always changing—but if your internal capabilities are strong, you can adjust to whatever happens.

All this makes me wonder: 3M is doing great, but obviously

many other companies out there also have a strong global presence yet are not doing so well in terms of coping with the pandemic. What are they doing wrong? What is another company of the same size, in the same industry, doing that isn't working? That thought in turn makes me wonder about *their* business model—not their current business model but the one they had before the pandemic hit, before any external factor ever affected them.

So what are these companies doing wrong? To answer that question, you have to go back to look at their *purpose*. Do they have one? What is their reason for existing? What value are they providing to their customers? Why is their firm uniquely capable of providing it? A company's purpose motivates their employees and clearly articulates and aligns strategic goals.

Having a really strong purpose and understanding the customer—having solid core strengths and understanding exactly what those are—are what enable companies to adapt quickly to whatever external threats may emerge.

Most companies don't look internally, but they should. They look at the external environment, and they are so focused on that environment that they forget to ask themselves, *What are our strengths and what can we do?*

Do Not Delay!

Most leaders today tend to procrastinate, looking for that *perfect* solution, but that solution usually isn't found right away. When external factors strike, speed is of the utmost importance. Just use what you have, lean in to your core strengths, and give it a try. You really can't go wrong if your current capabilities are strong. How well do you know your customers? How strong is your supply chain? And how well do you do operations?

You know what your core strengths are. Do you have good channels? Do you provide a good customer experience? Do you have a great value proposition? Whichever of these core strengths is the strongest, use that and see what you can do with it.

SCENARIO PLANNING

When you are formulating strategy, the planning process is usually undertaken a few months or maybe even up to a year in advance, depending on how big the strategy is. If it is a strategy for going into a brand-new market, it can take months to set up. And if you are doing something like that, you really need to engage in scenario planning or else you can lose that whole market. You will need to use the *techniques* of scenario planning that will help you spot early warning signs and organize your teams to take action on those insights.

Remember, I'm a microbiologist by education, and I used to work in labs before I worked my way up to corporate at Merck and got into supply chain management. From my time working in the lab, I know that scenario planning is part of the scientific mindset, and this approach governs everything that people in the science world do.

Science-related industries have practices that mimic what

we in the business world call *scenario planning*. These are the practices we use and the mindset we adopt in order to understand when we're dealing with something new.

"Something new" in scientific terms is analogous to a new external factor in business—a competitor's product that no one has ever seen before, a new market, a new president. These changes can create new entrepreneurial opportunities or result in damaging consequences for companies that operate under old assumptions or business models.

Anything that can potentially disrupt your supply chain management, such as riots, upheaval in your serving market, or an unanticipated "act of God," can cost you your competitive advantage when you need it most. It is useful to adapt your approaches and practices to mimic those that are already used in the science industry—to understand what works and what doesn't in order to determine how you'll need to adapt in the future.

Use Scenario Planning for Market Segments,
Not the Market as a Whole

When you use scenario planning, you want to make sure you are looking at the market in specific segments rather than in its entirety because if you are serving the Asia-Pacific market, the challenges you'll face are going to be very different from what you'll find in South America. From different demographics to different temperatures, there are endless differences in myriad factors that can affect supply chains.

Everything matters when you are looking at possible scenarios—the potential *what-ifs*. What if there is political instability and armed conflict in these places? Or what if there is a monsoon season?

For example, some years ago I was working with a company that made animal health products in the Asia-Pacific region—drugs and medicines for animals such as horses, cows, pigs, chickens, and whatnot. We were trying to increase efficiency in the supply chain to make sure we could meet demand, and this was a new market for us.

When you are looking at new markets, countless things can affect the supply chain: There could be a plant closure, or you could have a management crisis. You might have labor availability issues, or you could have infrastructure issues caused by a hurricane, a monsoon, or any number of things. And all these external factors will affect your service, your production costs, and your transportation costs.

It is important to focus on one segment at a time because you want to understand what *that segment* needs. When you are looking at Asia-Pacific markets, you are looking at China, you are looking at India, you are looking at Malaysia—but not every country is going to experience the same logistical challenges, and not every country is going to have the same amount of demand. So you want to look at it as a segment, and you want to create those *what-if* scenarios to determine what can happen that specifically is going to disrupt the supply chain to, say, Malaysia, whose COVID-related Restricted Movement Order has complicated business logistics, or to India due to monsoons.[8]

One of the things we did trying to serve this new market was to set up our strategy in such a way as to make sure we accounted for as many different scenarios as possible to ensure that our business model would not be interrupted—or that if it *were* interrupted, we would know what we could do to compensate. So we built scenarios that focused on data: how to spin out an effective forecast, how much animal medicine product we might have in the supply chain at any given time, what the production cost would be, and so on. The idea was to collect all the relevant supply chain data to make sure that our product actually got to where it was going safely and on time.

Seek Out Diverse Perspectives

When engaged in scenario planning, you want to share insights, and you want to make sure you have diverse perspectives on as many aspects of each scenario as possible.

When we were doing our scenario planning for the animal health company, we looked at different market perspectives; that is, we did market research and gathered a lot of consumer data. But what *really* helped us was that when we held our scenario planning sessions, we invited a lot of different people from a lot of different areas (not just people from the Asia-Pacific area) to come in and plan with us. We included the people who lived there and we had the business leaders who knew the market on the receiving end. One of the insights they gave us was that when there is a heavy monsoon season, sometimes the cows died from various diseases.

Now, here's the kicker. We didn't get that insight from any of the market research we paid for or from the formal interviews we conducted with logistics, transportation, and regulatory teams in places such as China and India, where they have monsoon seasons. But when we invited different local people to our scenario planning session, we discovered this insight.

Another reason you need to have a diverse group of people when doing scenario planning is that when you are working in a closed environment, you become more susceptible to confirmation bias. You think you know the market and have done a market litmus test, but you don't realize what other factors you may not have considered or what can change unexpectedly.

Scenario Planning Tools

Most companies already know that scenario planning works, but they're intimidated because they simply don't know how to do it. Today, however, digital tools make scenario planning really easy, so it can be done in a single workshop in a short time frame. These online tools enable people to gather virtually from all over the world without requiring them to come in personally.

* * *

In this book, I'll talk about innovation strategy and how you can build short- and long-term strategies by identifying growth opportunities and taking advantage of them. The work I do is kind of like teaching businesses how to run a marathon. It is a step-by-step process that starts by looking at who you are and where you are today, then brings you forward by helping you to innovate and make sure you have the right talent within your organization.

The mindset of a microbiologist and a scientist is such that when our work is disrupted by a microorganism, we don't look at it as a threat; rather, we see it as an opportunity to solve a problem. For all we know, the organism we are working with may help cure cancer. Or maybe it will just help grow your plants better. Whatever the case, the central question we ask is, *How can we use this organism to enhance our lives?*

That is the mindset of a scientist—when we see something new, whether it's adverse external factors affecting a business or microorganisms we have never seen before, we look at it as an opportunity to solve a problem.

If business leaders had that same mindset, maybe they wouldn't focus so intensely on the problems. They would look at these external factors as opportunities, not as threats.

In the rest of this book, I will discuss, among other topics,

- Being flexible so you can evolve with your customers and the market

- Letting go of your need for certainty, and cultivating an open mind, which can lead you to innovations

- Learning to embrace failure in your experiments and iteration process so you can innovate

2

BUILDING BRIDGES TO LUCRATIVE UNTAPPED MARKET SEGMENTS

The most important lesson I can share about brand marketing is this: you definitely, certainly, and surely don't have enough time and money to build a brand for everyone. You can't. Don't try. Be specific. Be very specific.

—SETH GODIN[1]

MORE

Every business wants—and needs—more of what makes it successful: more sales, more revenue, more prospects, more market share. A street vendor achieves happiness by selling out the day's supply of newspapers, water bottles, or what have you. He doesn't need to manage to the quarter or report higher earnings to Wall Street. But for managers in larger enterprises, it's always "grow or go." The surprising key to creating growth often lies outside one's current markets. In this chapter we'll explore a question that C-level executives often ask, "How do we enter new markets to find new arenas for growth where we've never before competed?"

Now, you may be thinking, *I'm doing well. Why should I change a business model that's working?* You're not alone. Most companies don't appreciate the urgency of broadening their market appeal—until some catastrophic event upends their relationship with their existing customers.

As I said in chapter 1, you need adaptability and drive to succeed. You need to be ready to adapt to change. And you must be looking at what's out there and considering how you can take advantage of undiscovered opportunities, even if your business is doing well.

Neglecting to explore new markets is a common mistake. In my experience working with C-level executives, they will often neglect to pursue new markets either because they think that doing so is unnecessary or because they don't know how. Yet as I demonstrate in this chapter, constantly exploring new markets is crucial to ensuring your lasting success.

HOW DO YOU DIFFERENTIATE YOUR PRODUCT IN A CROWDED MARKET?

Let me tell you about a social media campaign I launched for a well-known Fortune 500 dental care brand.

Dental care is a notoriously overcrowded market. Numerous big-name companies compete ferociously for market share in this space. So how do you differentiate a new product in a market like that, and how do you interest consumers in its key benefits?

In this case, that new product was designed to fight gingivitis—which made my job even more of a challenge because products designed to combat gingivitis are nearly as common as gingivitis itself; pretty much all dental care brands offer such products.

I find that research is key to creating a strong position for any new product so we identified and focused on a target audience: the health-focused individual looking to improve themselves every day. We wanted to reach men and women who are focused on making daily micro-improvements in their minds and bodies and who are looking for authentic natural ingredients in their food. They work out at the gym two to three times a week, and they also take time to meditate. This was our targeted customer.

First, we created a social media campaign to generate a visible fan base. Next, we made the product's presentation more powerful by introducing sleek new packaging we knew customers would love so we could differentiate our product on the shelf.

We also wanted to create a consumer experience to drive the trial, which we accomplished by placing display ads and giving out free samples at dental offices, supermarkets, and gyms.

What was the reasoning behind the placement of free trials at gyms? Remember, our target group is health-conscious individuals. Most people who work out at a gym have an established, habitual morning and evening routine, so the idea was to make sure that our messaging reminded them to brush their teeth in the morning and before going to bed. We wanted to get them thinking, while brushing, about which brand they use for their dental care needs. When the consumer is at the gym, she notices the display; maybe she takes a free sample and maybe she doesn't. But either way, when she's brushing her teeth later that night, she'll remember that display and wonder whether she has a gingivitis problem—and that's what puts us on her radar.

We also created video ads that described the habits of a healthy, focused person—that is, how they improve their lives. Our core strength was our messaging about making daily micro-improvements in the mind and body. Just as we exercise and are mindful about the kinds of foods we put in our bodies, we also need to be conscious of our dental health as we get older—and so the message was that brushing with this specific brand of toothpaste should be part of a regimen to build good dental health over time.

Finally, we partnered with dental experts to promote the new product and explain its value. Instead of just thinking about the direct consumer sales with our current business model, we recruited advocates—not just dentists but also trainers at the gyms—and then created engagements on various social media platforms to amplify our message. We set up kiosk stations at places such as Costco and BJ's Wholesale Club, and we offered free samples at organic grocery chains such as Whole Foods and Trader Joe's and at local grocery stores selling organic foods.

This enabled us to broadcast a consistent message: dental care needs to be part of your routine if you're concerned about your overall health—and using this specific product, from this specific brand, is key to realizing the benefits of having a healthy lifestyle. The campaign resulted in reaching twenty million people online, 60 percent ad recall, 23 percent uplift in consideration, and three times more growth compared to its category.

USING SEGMENTATION TO DRIVE GROWTH

The 2008 financial crisis was a public relations disaster that put a lot of pressure on wealth management firms, banks, and other arms of the financial industry to rebuild consumer trust—an ongoing task that may take decades.

I recently worked with a firm that provides financial planning and wealth management services for individuals and business owners. This firm wanted to use segmentation to drive growth and acquire new customers, and they told me, "Bella, we're looking at millennials."

What comes to mind when we think of millennials? Well, they are more tech savvy than previous generations—they use their smartphones much more than they use any other device, and they use a lot of on-demand services. Millennials also care a lot about reliability, quality, customer service, and transparency.

This financial firm viewed millennials as an undertapped market they could serve. I suggested that going after millennials as a whole would be painting with too broad a brush. The firm needed to see how they could segment this market. In other words, they wanted to find out *which* segments of millennials they should go after (or whether they really should just go after millennials as a whole).

To successfully segment millennials, we needed to see who the millennials *are*. The word *millennial* encompasses many different groups, or segments: millennial business owners, unemployed millennials, single millennials, recently married millennials, and so on. Which segments, we wondered, would turn out to be our ideal targets?

We started by reviewing market research that the firm had already done to find out what information was missing. From that, we built an integrated view of the customer. First, we identified a variety of characteristics, attitudes, and behaviors typical of different millennials. From there we created a detailed map of how those segments related to different stakeholders within the organization. For example, within the firm one individual specialized in business taxes and another person focused on estate planning. The goal was to align these segments with the different financial functions of the organization to make sure we could serve these people if they became our customers—that is, we ensured they were the right segments to go after.

Then we started to think about how these segments might

connect to our existing customers and whether we could use them to engage with and guide millennials into thinking about long-term planning.

At this point, we were ready to identify the segments and subsegments of our market. We wanted groups for whom we could craft hypertargeted messaging—without alienating any of the general market the firm already served. Our independent research led us to conclude that we wanted to focus on two very specific millennial segments: Asian American business owners and recently married couples.

We chose the first segment, Asian American business owners, for several reasons. First, this firm does financial planning for a specific market—individuals, and especially business owners, who earn more than $5 million a year. We knew from our market research that Asian American millennials are one of America's fastest-growing populations and have very strong purchasing power.

As for the second segment, our independent research showed that married millennials, on average, have more than $100,000 in investable assets. They are financially confident, love personalization, are socially connected, and have entrepreneurial aspirations.

SEGMENTATION MAKES YOU MORE ADAPTABLE

Most companies don't conduct segmentation and niche marketing, perhaps because their philosophy is that they want the broadest possible market for their offerings. Yet for those that put the effort in, the rewards are manifold. For starters, segmentation marketing makes you more adaptable. Let me explain why.

The wealth management firm I was working with understood that they were going to have to be adaptable to whatever this new segment might need. Unlike other companies that become set in their ways while serving a narrow customer base, companies that pursue segmentation are forced to adapt to the needs of different customers. This firm therefore worked to discover what their millennial prospects might require for the firm's platform to better connect with them and became more flexible in the process.

This wealth management firm was willing to focus on a niche strategy to better understand the market, but most companies are not. Instead, most companies focus only on sales. This is a mistake that prevents companies from positioning themselves to really own specific market segments. When you spend a lot of time building a specific segment, learning their behaviors and whom they know and what they want, it helps you to figure out how to provide the best service to them. This helps you become more adaptable and flexible as you grow your existing market segment. At the same time, it fosters stability, thereby building a strong foundation for your new market segments.

CREATING CHAIN REACTIONS THROUGH SEGMENTATION

In my work with the wealth management firm, we picked millennial Asian business owners in part because of their strong purchasing power. But they are also a segment that can create entry points into other segments, potentially giving us access to other prospective millennial customers.

Although you have two different segments that will receive two different types of messaging, a chain reaction can occur through word of mouth. Dr. Jonah Berger, a best-selling author and marketing professor at the Wharton School of the University of Pennsylvania, says that social currency (feeling like an insider) and triggers can be used in marketing messages to get your customers to share your products or services with others.[2]

When one of our segment programs is doing better, we can learn from it and devise ways to improve and promote another program as well. To that end, we created an online platform to connect that financial firm's prospective millennial clients with their existing Generation X and baby boomer clientele, who could draw on their experience and offer coaching or mentorship.

Once you start looking for them, the opportunities for such chain reactions become surprisingly visible everywhere. The emerging wave of start-ups across local cities has created a new benchmark for inclusion across banking, validating the new campaigns and acquisition of new clients.

A DIFFERENT WAY TO SEGMENT POTENTIAL MARKETS

If you follow health food crazes, you may have heard of a new "superfood," a plant called moringa, that has been used for thousands of years in Indian cooking and in traditional Indian Ayurveda medicine. Although moringa is new to the United

States (it has become popular only in the last five years or so), I am familiar with it because I'm from India. The plant grows in India and also in Africa. So what's new in the West is something that other parts of the world have known for centuries.

Moringa is full of nutrients and antioxidants: protein, vitamin B6, vitamin C, iron, riboflavin, vitamin A, and magnesium. It is said to relieve inflammation, and it also lowers blood sugar and cholesterol, among other health benefits. Yet very few US companies are producing or importing it. I'm working with an international client who is bringing moringa to the United States. When I started working with this client, my marketing assignment was to build an activation plan to increase awareness of this product and demand for it. The question arises: How do you create awareness of a product such as this? How do you reach audiences who are into healthy eating and educate them about this product so that they learn more about it and buy it?

When a company introduces a new category of superfood in the United States, the initial target market comprises athletes, gyms or gym employees, and eventually chains such as Whole Foods and organic stores specifically geared toward selling these kinds of products. Ever since Whole Foods first appeared, it has been an easy entry point for organic and plant-based foods. And we know that in-store channels are the fastest way to increase awareness to sell these products.

Our research indicated that 33 percent of millennials, ages twenty-one to thirty-four, said health attributes were important to them and they were willing to pay premium prices for these types of foods. We also knew from research that reduced packaging size was trending at the time and that there had been huge growth in single-person households in recent years.

In today's world, we have enormous amounts of research that focus on consumer sensory cues and behavioral techniques. The insights gleaned from this research help us understand why consumers do what they do, so we know how to define a given segment and how to market to that group.

Armed with this information, I took a different approach to segmenting. Instead of using the same kind of hypersegmentation I'd done with the wealth management organization, ferreting out one specific target group, we targeted all our prospects by using a database of different types of segments that are already in the market. This strategy identified anyone who might be interested in the product. We used a software database to figure out which type of segments might include a healthy person interested in eating moringa as a supplement, drinking moringa as a powder mixed with water, or eating moringa snack bars. So what kind of population—what kind of segment—are we looking at?

Using this database approach, we were able to create segments based on the performance of the messaging with various groups. We created test messaging to target individuals who might be interested in this product. Instead of identifying a traditional segment or a persona—say, a yoga instructor between the ages of twenty-four to thirty-five who wants to pay premium prices for healthy living—we used a lot of different data sets about general consumers and were able to create many different segments from that.

This approach is important when doing segmentation of new markets, and it's especially valuable for a newer company (less than three years old) looking to create awareness of its product. Newer businesses need to focus on raising awareness of the product and making sure it is relevant to the consumer so that they can determine how their brand can stay relevant as time passes.

As we gained more insight about these segments, we started to cluster them according to variables such as lifestyle, age, and demographics. We created messaging specific to those two or three segments from which we'd received the most insight, and then we activated a marketing plan to deliver a ROI. This is how a broader segmenting approach can be used to first explore and then target new markets.

Obviously, we start with the market that exists today for a given product—but what about tomorrow? When gathering information, you are looking at both the present and the future. As you're building your business, you want to focus on understanding the *other* segments you can reach—the ones you didn't target the first time around. This means you are simultaneously strengthening your business model with current segments, working to build new segments, and collecting data for *future* business. This will help the company create a stronger foundation and be more innovative and adaptable to changing consumer needs. We created a comprehensive communication framework that would deliver to our segments. The campaign produced an uplift of 123 percent in brand interest, product interest, and purchase intent and consideration.

HOW NINTENDO GOT LUCKY WITH *ANIMAL CROSSING*—
TWENTY YEARS AFTER ITS LAUNCH

Readers who are video game aficionados may be familiar with a Nintendo game called *Animal Crossing*. The game, which debuted in 2001, was designed for children, and it features the kind of anthropomorphic "funny animal" characters that children like.

Interestingly, recent research indicates that 40 percent of *Animal Crossing*'s sales are now made to *adult* female players—most probably women who started playing this game with their children but then got hooked on playing it themselves when the COVID-19 pandemic forced us all to spend endless hours at home looking for things to do.

In December 2020, I got a Christmas card from a neighbor in her late fifties. In her family Christmas card, she described how she passed the pandemic playing *Animal Crossing* online, and she talked about the friendships she made.

Animal Crossing, from a business perspective, could be called *Segment Crossing* because the game so effectively expanded beyond its original intended target of preteens and teenagers. Nintendo now has new markets and new segments: people who have been stuck at home.

You might ask what we've learned from the COVID/ *Animal Crossing* story. Wasn't it just blind luck that a twenty-year-old game found a new audience during a once-in-a-lifetime (we hope!) pandemic? It's true that Nintendo did not display strategic intent while developing a hard-core following of homebound fiftysomethings. But *Animal Crossing* is succeeding in these trying times because the game addresses three basic human needs: *autonomy, competence*, and *relatedness*.

A June 2020 article in *Science Focus* magazine notes this aspect of the video game and talks about the science behind its success and why it became so popular with all ages.

First, autonomy: In the game, you can build your own house and spend your money on whatever you want. It lets you go fishing, do arts and crafts, and even invest in the stock market—in whatever stocks *you* want to pick. Second, you use your growing competence at the game to invest in yourself. Finally, there is relatedness—being able to relate yourself with others. When you're playing the game, you're connecting with your neighbors. You can play online with friends. Your neighbors can give you gifts. They can come over, talk to you, and even send mail to someone through the game!

Science Focus connects this to the concept of "Self-Determination Theory" and posits it as the reason the game became so successful so quickly:

First developed in the 1980s by psychologists Edward Deci and Richard Ryan, Self-Determination Theory suggests that while some behaviors are driven by external motivation (say, to gain a reward such as money or praise), others are shaped by more intrinsic forms of motivation—that is, we do some things simply because we enjoy them.[3]

We can look to the great 1980s philosopher Cyndi Lauper, who said it best: sometimes, girls (and guys, too!) just want to have fun.

From a business perspective, the results Nintendo achieved are impressive, even if they were unintentional. The company had developed a game that not only targeted young people but also met these three basic human needs. This gave them a real edge during the pandemic when these needs were otherwise not being met (even if they couldn't have predicted that). Going forward, the development of that market segment will give Nintendo an edge in reaching many new markets in the future.

Any business can learn from Nintendo's good fortune. The lesson isn't "Put out a product, wait twenty years, and hope for the best." Instead, the real lesson of *Animal Crossing* is that you can find new market segments if your business meets one of the three human needs that *Animal Crossing* accidentally addressed.

Autonomy

You can address this need by providing consumers with digital customization tools that make life easier and more convenient. If you manufacture refrigerators, perhaps your new refrigerators have a built-in Alexa connection. Or maybe they have an ice maker that allows the consumer to decide, "I want my ice to be in heart shapes." Autonomy is what enables *you* to customize, to pick and choose the features you want.

Consider an example from the auto industry: A woman shopping for a car came to an auto show seeking a particular model—a really expensive one. She wanted the car in a very specific color. When the dealer asked, "What color do you want it in?" she replied, "I want it the same color as my nail polish."

In a masterstroke of salesmanship, he asked for and received a piece of her nail with the polish on it and brought it back to the manufacturer. The manufacturer built her a car in that exact color! (This story was told in Robin Sharma's online course, Personal Mastery Academy Online, in a discussion about how one car company obsesses over its customers.[4])

Customization and personalization don't get better than that. It's giving your customers the opportunity to pick what they want and supporting them in getting it. We've come a long way from Henry Ford saying, "Customers can buy our cars in any color they want . . . as long as it's black!"

Competence

In early 2020, Johnson & Johnson Consumer Health launched the Nicorette QuickMist SmartTrack app, which is designed to enable consumers to create personalized plans to quit smoking. The app tracks the consumer's usage of Nicorette QuickMist and monitors milestones and money saved by not buying cigarettes. By doing this, SmartTrack provides motivation and encouragement and addresses the difficulty of seeing day-to-day progress in one's attempt to quit smoking.[5] The brand is committed to helping people prioritize today over tomorrow by encouraging them with a sense of empowerment and motivation through socially conforming in the community. They do this by recognizing pro-social behavior on their own behalf as well as highlighting it when they see others doing it too.

Relatedness

During the pandemic crisis, we saw ads focused on human connection, especially to local communities. For example, Michael's Makers, an arts and crafts supply company, transformed their business within a few weeks to offer curbside pickup and partnered with UPS to offer same-day delivery service for their customers. Many luxury brands, including Prada and LVMH, have repurposed their factories and other resources to make pandemic-related necessities such as hand sanitizer and masks.[6] And Budweiser's emotional "One Team" ad paid tribute to everyday heroes working during the pandemic. Dove shifted its focus from confidence to courage that is aligned with its beauty purpose. They launched a campaign called *Courage Is Beautiful* that highlighted health care heroes on social media by posting pictures of them exhausted but also bruised in order to show how beautiful they are despite everything going against them during the pandemic's emergency situation. By using courage as an attribute, this campaign created a connection with the community amid pandemic circumstances. This allowed increased engagement on social media channels all over the world![7]

By intentionally attending to these three basic needs—autonomy, competence, and relatedness—you will win more loyal, long-term customers.

* * *

When we look at new markets and new segments, we need to think about today *and* tomorrow. What is the business model today? And what can it be tomorrow with these segments, these new markets?

Obviously we don't know what tomorrow will look like. That is why we collect data. This is crucial because it gives us insight into market changes as they begin to happen. We position ourselves to notice new trends, new buying patterns, and market segments with increasing purchasing power. We get better insight into our current customers and their changing needs so we can keep up with them and continue to serve them. At the same time, we discover untapped markets for our products and find ways to reach them.

Identifying and capturing the market segment you want to go after today is not the end of the story. If that's all you are relying on, someone else will find a way to take those millennial Asian American business owners away from *your* firm and bring them over to *theirs*. What are you doing to stay relevant? When unforeseen external events such as the COVID-19 pandemic arise, how are you going to adjust? How will you keep your customers, and how will you continue to serve them better? My advice: collect data for tomorrow and use that information to build better solutions for your existing and future customers. This will help you grow your brand, grow your products and services, and grow your markets.

We need to think about these things when building a business model. Although we can't imagine what tomorrow will look like, we can do everything in our power to be ready for it. We've talked in this chapter about tapping into new market segments. In the next chapter, we'll discuss smart ways to leverage digital technology to drive engagement with subscription models in order to create sustainable, predictable revenue that will carry you through whatever tomorrow's challenges turn out to be.

KEY TAKEAWAYS

- Constantly exploring new markets is crucial to ensuring success.

- Be specific: segmentation marketing makes you more adaptable.

- Connecting with a new market segment can create entry points into other segments.

- Addressing three basic human needs—autonomy, competence, and relatedness—helps a business win loyal, long-term customers.

3

SUBSCRIPTION MODELS AND THE "INTERNET OF THINGS"

The innovations are far more important because the technology itself has no way to impact the world for good until it's embedded in the business model. Innovation is the combination of the simplifying technology and the business model.

—CLAYTON CHRISTENSEN[1]

WHEN A COMPANY has experienced a long period of sustained growth, it is common to look back and reflect on its growth strategy over time in order to evaluate what works and what doesn't. Usually a company engaged in this sort of reflection is looking to improve its delivery methods or customer service.

But that is not enough.

In today's hypercompetitive environment, you need to form ongoing relationships with your customers rather than be content with a single sale. Today the name of the game is *engagement*. To that end, many companies are now leveraging digital technology to ensure that the customer relationship doesn't end with one interaction or one transaction.

In this chapter I want to talk about subscription models and how you can use technology to drive engagement, thereby building a new business model that will enable you to better serve your market.

That, in turn, helps you to maintain the solid footing you need in order to prepare for the unexpected curveballs life will inevitably throw at you.

THE BENEFITS OF A SUBSCRIPTION MODEL

Subscription has become something of a business buzzword in recent years because subscription income is regular and repeatable. You don't have to keep making sale after sale; rather, the subscription itself is a sale that repeats on a regular basis.

Everybody wants that, but many businesses don't feel they have a path to creating subscription income. That's too bad, because income that you can count on month after month not only benefits you on a day-to-day basis in the here and now but also makes a business saleable—and therefore more valuable—in the long run.

A good subscription model will focus on one (or more) of four benefits to the consumer: convenience, quality, the possibility of discovering new products, and simplicity.

Let's first look at convenience. Think of streaming services such as Disney+ or Netflix, which offer a near-limitless selection of movies without you ever having to go out to spend thirty dollars at a theater. Or consider NordicTrack, which enables you to get your workouts in at home, through a screen, rather than trudging all the way down to a noisy gym filled with sweaty machines that somebody else didn't bother to wipe down after using.

The second benefit is the quality of the products that can be offered by a high-end subscription-based business: think of all those online meal services that deliver fresh food and recipes straight to your home—companies such as Sunbasket and Blue Apron. Not only do we have convenience but there's also a quality factor—the subscription-based model employed by Sunbasket and Blue Apron enables them to deliver a higher-quality product by allowing them to better allocate their resources to provide fresh ingredients since they already have a heads-up on future orders.

These meal services also provide consumers with the benefit of discovering new products. Dollar Shave Club offers a subscription model through which the company has extended its product line to offer not just blades but other shaving essentials and even bar soaps and hair products. This service gives Dollar Shave Club the flexibility to introduce new products and test new ideas.

The fourth benefit of any good subscription plan is its simplicity. If the plan is attractively simple (i.e., it doesn't look like a big hassle to get involved with), then customers are more likely to be interested in signing up. And simplicity can translate to adaptability in the long run.

Amazon excels at simplicity. If you're ordering the same item from them on a regular basis, you can choose onetime delivery or opt to "Subscribe and Save." For example, if I have a dog, choosing this option means I don't have to remember when to order dog food every month—and therefore I don't have to risk opening the pantry one day to find there is no dog food in the house. It is automatically delivered right when I need it. Even better, if I subscribe to five or more monthly product deliveries, Amazon will offer me a 15 percent discount.[2] And I can always make changes to my dog food order with a simple mouse click if I need to. It's a very simple process, and that is why it works.

Subscription services are rapidly becoming a common business model, and the concept has crossed over to nearly every industry—everything from airlines to cars to the food industry.

Looking at the car industry, for example, we see that Volvo offers an all-inclusive subscription model that allows you to lease a car on a monthly basis with insurance, maintenance, and roadside assistance included. And of course you can cancel if you decide you don't want to drive that Volvo anymore—which is much easier than selling and replacing a car you bought outright.

Porsche recently came up with a subscription leasing model of their own: if you lease one of their cars, you have the option to change your selection as often as you want—even every week, if you like. So this week you could be driving a blue Porsche 911, and next week you could be driving a red Panamera or Boxster. You can even choose a multivehicle subscription and keep multiple different Porsches in your driveway to impress the neighbors. (And of course, there is white-glove delivery.)

CUSTOMER LIFETIME VALUE

The next important thing I want to talk about with respect to strategy is *customer lifetime value* (CLV).

Customer lifetime value is a metric for predicting the total revenue from a customer over the lifetime of their relationship to your business and for tracking retention rates. If you are considering a subscription model, you need to have some idea what the retention rate is going to be. Is the customer going to be satisfied with this new way of doing things or will they want to go back to the old business model?

The CLV metric looks at customer acquisition, retention, the average lifetime number of transactions, and the cost to serve the customer over the lifetime of the relationship. For our purpose here (evaluating the potential of a subscription model), the key element to look at is the retention rate.

Once you've conducted some pilot testing—and after you've looked at CLV and carefully examined consumer behavior—you'll have a better understanding of what you need to do before you start reaching out to the bigger market. You'll know what works and how you are going to implement your subscription model.

These are important steps to take if you want to prevent a situation in which your customer can't easily use your subscription model or isn't interested. This is why you want to test it with your existing market and constantly be collecting data. Testing the initiative with your existing customer base is the key to creating a framework that will help you develop a deeper understanding of and relationship with your customers.

SUBSCRIPTION MODELS AND COLLECTING DATA VIA THE IoT

In addition to providing predictable revenue, another benefit to the subscription model—indeed, possibly one of its most important benefits—is that it allows you to work directly with the customer and therefore collect lots of data on them. A subscription service provides you with the opportunity to track customer behavior, which enables you to tweak your products and services and constantly make improvements.

For a subscription model to be successful, you need to focus on consumer behavior, not the actual product or service you're delivering. Don't worry so much about the latter. Your service is already good; that's why they're signing up for it.

Instead, you should focus on monitoring your customers' behaviors so you can make improvements to your product in the future when their needs may be different. You need to understand what motivates them, what drives them to action. You also need to understand current trends—but be aware that those trends can change very quickly. What people are doing today may not interest them tomorrow. It is therefore *very* important that you gather data.

Collecting data directly from your subscribers is one way to do this; of course, you're probably doing that anyway in the normal course of customer acquisition, in addition to other traditional methods such as market research and focus groups.

But there's another, often overlooked way to collect customer data: IoT sensors.

In case you're not familiar with the term, *IoT* stands for the "Internet of Things." The term refers to the network of people to people, people to things, and things to things. It includes components of machines, electronics, personal devices, and anything that can be connected with the Internet.[3]

For example, a smart fridge knows when you're almost out of milk and may even be able to tell that your eggs have gone bad—and can place an order for you online without you having to take any action at all. (Yes, such things really do exist![4]) The devices that enable your fridge to collect this information are called IoT sensors.

To give you an idea of how this technology can be employed in the service of a subscription model, I want to talk about an assignment I once had to develop a data-driven subscription model for a medical device company.

This company provides various medical devices and machines to hospitals for use in surgery. If we wanted to persuade those hospitals to switch to a subscription model, we would have to figure out how to overcome certain adoption barriers: Why should a hospital convert to a subscription model rather than simply buying the machines outright or renting them on an ad hoc basis? They need the devices anyway. They are going to order them. What is the benefit of a subscription model?

The insight we had is that the customers want to be in control. They want to have choices, and they want to be able to select their own products and features and decide on the time line of delivery. For this medical device company, we created a subscription business model similar to a traditional medical equipment lease, but we leveraged technology to make the system work better both for the company and its customers, the hospitals.

This is where the tech comes in and things get interesting—because this is where the data collection happens. We have sensors embedded in the medical equipment that send data to the operating room staff on a mobile app. Using this app, the surgeons or staff can see which devices are available before the surgery they want to perform, and they can even see what specific model is available, in what size, and what features it has. This information can also be sent to the medical device company so it can track its customers' usage: Which devices are they actually using, and which ones are just sitting there? How long before they need to order a new one?

Using design thinking methods, we assigned teams to collect customer behavior data on how the medical components are used. We set up surveys and on-site interviews with observations for a two-week period. Our team was able to collect insights, test rapid prototyping, and conduct ongoing testing to tackle complex challenges. Based on our findings we created a problem-solving approach that included empathy mapping sessions and usability tests with sales reps and hospital staff. This helped us understand the pain points to create new prototypes that were tested over several weeks by staff and our teams. We could not rely on the IoT data alone to meet the needs of the hospital staff. The idea was to truly understand how certain surgical components were being used by operating room staff members in complex cases and to build a relationship with the customer based on their usage.

We learned from our pilot testing how various medical components are used, how often they are delivered, and which procedures use the same components every time. Collecting this data enables the medical device company to predict needs and recommend the right quantity of each component for the hospital to order. This key piece of information enables the hospital to better manage inventory and save space—that is, to avoid having too much unnecessary equipment lying around.

You can also use the CLV metric to evaluate new initiatives and performance benchmarks over time. That means that if you're looking to introduce a new component to the doctor through your sales team, you can actually predict when would be a good time to do that. When you start to see nonusage in a certain type of component or that they have changed the way they do surgery and certain devices are not used as much anymore (or are now used somewhere else), you know when you can try to introduce something new.

Using CLV for forecasting future purchases also allows the medical device company to be well informed when introducing new products to the market, and it allows for benchmarking with market size and adjustments to pricing strategies.

By leveraging technology and using IoT sensors, you collect data that shows how you can make your subscription business model better. This is not just a typical subscription model where you pay X dollars and get X number of devices and components for the hospital. This is about providing a service rather than a product: you are providing confidence that their patients' surgeries will go well. You are providing confidence to the doctor that he or she will be able to have the right equipment and components in place, and you are saving on inventory space in the bargain.

Returns of unused medical devices and components are very common for medical device companies. Why does that happen? Those devices and components could be sent to another hospital or some other place where they could be used. Who is keeping track of all that? The salespeople are generally involved in making that first sale, and then the surgeons have to make ad hoc requests to ensure that they have the equipment they need to perform that week's surgeries. Much of that equipment is sent in bulk, according to some administrator's estimate of how many components they are going to use this year. And when they don't end up using it or you are returning it, what happens then? Why aren't those devices being used?

An IoT platform-monitored subscription model answers those questions and therefore benefits both the customer (in terms of cost) and the medical device company (in terms of understanding what products it should focus on). Also, the implementation of this IoT strategy creates a link to company databases and hospital database systems using API, which becomes part of the operating infrastructure. The only problem is that it can be difficult or expensive to replace when necessary because of its integration into operations. However, the long-term benefits are worth the investment!

Now, I don't want you to get the idea that any of this is specific to the medical device industry. The IoT also includes smart home security systems, biometric cybersecurity scanners, smart factory equipment, and so much more. The value of this kind of tech-augmented subscription model is universal. It can be used in most industries as long as it provides benefit and ease to the customer. For example, John Deere, the agricultural company, uses IoT sensors to collect data that helps farmers monitor how many seeds they're planting per acre and even measure how much pressure is being put on those seeds as they're being placed. They can also track the vehicles themselves—the tractors, plows, and other farming equipment John Deere makes—to determine whether they're operating properly and what services they may need. The legendary farm-equipment manufacturer's factory operations now employ an industrial IoT platform "to collect and analyze real-time assembly information to improve line efficiency, prevent unplanned downtime, and improve efficiency throughout the supply chain."[5]

Beyond IoT sensors, other forms of technology are also being implemented. "We are seeing the emergence of productivity-boosting concepts such as artificial intelligence and machine learning," said John Deere CEO John May. "These technologies have game-changing promise in terms of improving yields and making more efficient use of fertilizers, herbicides and other chemicals. Decisions once made at the field level are evolving to section level, row level, even to the plant level."[6]

CREATING FLEXIBLE THINKING TO ACHIEVE PREDICTABILITY

Predictability and flexible thinking—that's what this is all about. That's what a subscription model gives you. How can I create new relationships? What is the retention likelihood for this customer? How likely are they to use our product before we need to worry about new innovations or improvements? How can we make the customer's life so predictable—and therefore so easy—that they remain loyal for years or decades? And how can we leverage that loyalty, in turn, to provide that same sweet predictability to our own business? Can we create third-party services leveraging other connected devices and provide customization for our customers?

That kind of predictability is what allows you to serve your customers better. A data-driven subscription model is what gives you that advantage because it enables you to predict what your *future* customers will want from you.

Predictability comes from the ability to forecast demand, which enables you to offer a better product and a better service. And by providing your customer with that predictive confidence, you get them excited about your brand. That's what *motivates* the customer. Therefore you have to constantly remind them of who you are and why they signed up with you in the first place.

It needs to be about more than a great medical component or a device. Customers should think, *Wow, they made my life easier*. Now you can shift your focus and say, "Okay, what else can we provide for this customer? What else can we offer them? Maybe I can add new, higher-level features to my subscription and even make more money. What can I do for them? What do they like? What are their behaviors?" Building on delivering a consistent customer experience, staying connected with them, and providing value is a great way to increase customer loyalty.

Learning the answers to these questions helps you understand your customers' behavior, and that in turn will strengthen your subscription model. With the right kind of technology, you can produce a high-quality product for your customers at the right time—and that's all you need to do to keep them loyal for life.

Business leaders need to move away from excessive focus on ROI and concentrate instead on understanding their customers. They need to manage differently in order to have the flexibility to introduce new business models that better address customers' needs. Like a street vendor, they need to embrace organizational flexibility that enables them to explore new options to meet the requirements of a rapidly evolving marketplace.

In the next chapter, we're going to talk about something else I never had as a street vendor: access to faraway markets!

KEY TAKEAWAYS

- In a hypercompetitive environment, you need to form ongoing relationships with your customers rather than being content with a single sale.

- A good subscription model will focus on one or more of four benefits to the consumer: convenience, quality, the possibility of discovering new products, and simplicity.

- By leveraging technology and using IoT sensors, you can fundamentally change the business model to reduce cost and improve operating efficiencies.

4

EXPLORING NEW MARKETS

Marketing takes a day to learn and a lifetime to master.

—Philip Kotler[1]

ONE OF THE BEST WAYS to ensure that your company is prepared to deal with unexpected external events is to expand into new markets whenever possible—both domestically and overseas. Just as my childhood as a street vendor required my family to be flexible enough to move down a few blocks if a road closure was affecting our usual location, your company can benefit from having other sources of revenue if a recession or natural disaster interrupts or reduces revenue from your primary market. Flexibility and resiliency are important qualities for any company. That's why it's critical that you build other sources of revenue into your business plan so if a recession or natural disaster disrupts the primary market where buyers are located, the company can continue operating without interruption while awaiting recovery efforts.

Jumping into a new market, however—whether domestic or foreign—is not something to be undertaken lightly. When moving from one continent to another, or even simply from one US metro area to another, you will encounter cultural differences and logistical issues that can easily trip you up and ruin your plans. Consumer behavior will differ from one place to another, as will local laws, economic conditions, infrastructure, and so on.

Whether you should expand domestically or internationally depends on the size and objectives of the organization. If you are a small or midsized company—if you don't have the resources of a large corporation and don't have many employees—it is going to be harder for you to go global. You may not have enough manpower to collect and analyze the data you need, much less to send people out there to start something new.

Global expansion is really for companies that have been around for a long time—like ten-plus years. A large corporation has the funding it needs; it has the resources and manpower and can leverage those to create partnerships faster and collaborate with other companies much more efficiently because people know who it is. This makes it easier for it to find an entry point.

If you're a small company, I advise you to try your neighboring state or even your neighboring city before you start expanding nationally. You want to create more awareness, you need an online presence, and you want to have diverse talent first. You should always experiment in your own country before you try going global.

In this chapter I'll show you how to navigate these challenges—what to expect and how to mitigate the negative consequences of the mistakes you will inevitably make along the way. I'll also show you how to adjust your messaging and strategy accordingly while holding to the core values of your brand.

MAKING THE DECISION

The first question to consider, of course, is whether to move into a particular new market. What criteria should inform that decision?

First, you want to look at whether there is a *demand* in this market for your product or service. Can you address any pain points in that market, and does a significant portion of the population feel that pain? (If not, then the minimal prospective gains probably aren't worth the effort and expense you'd have to invest.)

The next thing to consider is *infrastructure*. This is a huge concern, especially in less-developed regions such as India or Africa. Some of these emerging markets don't even have good roads. If you are distributing a product and your trucks can't reach the distribution center because the roads are poorly developed, you're going to have a huge problem moving inventory.

Moreover, in any country with problematic roads, these kinds of infrastructural deficiencies are going to extend to other areas. You may find yourself having to contend with poorly built factories with substandard wiring and plumbing; unreliable public transportation that your employees depend on to get to work; unsafe vehicles, machinery, and warehouse equipment; and so on. These problems may not be insurmountable, and if the demand is there, the grief may be worth it and then some—but you need to be clear-eyed about what you're getting into.

Bear in mind that the seriousness of the infrastructure question may depend on whether you're selling a physical product as opposed to a service. Service platforms often do really well no matter where they go: when companies such as Facebook go to India, for example, they are usually up and running pretty quickly compared to companies that have to bring in physical products, such as Coca-Cola or Toyota. (Of course, both *those* companies have been operating globally for many years, but even they have had initial challenges to overcome in every new market they ever entered.)

The exact nature of the challenges you'll face in any new market is unknowable, so it's prudent to engage local partners who can give you the lay of the land. You need someone to give you *insight*, someone who can tell you which neighborhoods are most likely to respond to what you're offering or which populations may be too difficult to reach, either because of infrastructure issues or a lack of foreseeable public interest. So *opportunities for collaboration and partnerships* are among the first things you should look for.

The last thing to look at is *regulation*. This is a big one, especially if your product or service is heavily regulated here at home—for example, pharmaceutical companies. You have to make sure you are in compliance with local laws and regulations governing whatever kind of medicine you're bringing in and ensure you have the necessary documentation and approvals.

More broadly than that, you need to consider the overall regulatory environment of your prospective new market. If it's too restrictive, you may find yourself endlessly paying exorbitant fees for licenses to operate various aspects of your business. If the regulatory environment is too lax, on the other hand, this may be an indication that the rule of law in that country is too weak for you to do business safely—your intellectual property may not be well protected or there may be crime problems, violence, costly government corruption, and so on.

GETTING STARTED

Again, your first question should be, *Is there a demand for my product or service in that market?* Based on my experience as a consultant, I'd say that eight out of ten times the answer is *yes*. Unless you have a unique niche product or service that is not applicable to the market you're looking at, there will probably be a demand—after all, human beings all over the world need and use the same services and products.

Research: Getting the Lay of the Land

How do you get to know a market and understand the landscape? The first requirement is research. A big business will have money to hire a research firm to go in and get actual firsthand insights. The CEO of a large corporation can contact a research company and say, "I want you to research the following types of products and the following types of segments in India. What is our brand image there? Is there a need in that market that our product or service can address?"

Research can be bought in this way, or you can produce it in-house by sending your own people to observe whatever market you've got your eye on. In his insightful book *The Greatest Business Decisions of All Time*, Verne Harnish tells the story of how, in the early 1990s, Samsung CEO Lee Kun-hee sent his sales reps to live in various locations around the world—to learn the local languages and cultures and how people used technology there—in order to determine how Samsung could supply those markets.[2]

Your pockets may not be deep enough for such a large-scale global information-collection project. But if you're able to send a small team into a potential new market, you should do so. Give your units and divisions the freedom to explore that market a little bit. Have them meet with local business leaders and government officials and ask questions. Provide them the resources, tools, and money to be able to collect whatever information they need, to hire people if necessary, and to form partnerships with local talent who can help them understand what the market is really about. This gives you clearer customer insights, allowing you to develop better and bigger partnerships to connect better with your customers.

You can't just rush in and plant yourself and say, "Okay, we're a global brand, and everybody knows who we are, so people are inevitably going to stampede to buy our product." It doesn't work that way. The better strategy is to attach yourself to someone who is already enmeshed in the local culture, to form a relationship that allows you to piggyback on legwork that has already been done. This provides an entry point that allows you to grow your brand naturally.

One of the best tools for this kind of "piggyback" strategy is the *startup incubator*.

According to the US Chamber of Commerce, "A startup incubator is a collaborative program for startup companies . . . designed to help startups in their infancy succeed by providing workspace, seed funding, mentoring and training."[3]

Startup incubators are very popular in Europe and Asia where local communities endorse and sponsor aspiring entrepreneurs. The idea is to look for start-ups in your new market that are working on a technology or a service that is relevant to your company. You can partner with an existing incubator—or you can provide your own incubation services.

Your relationship with a local entrepreneur will benefit both of you. The entrepreneur and his or her start-up benefit from your patronage, mentorship, and funding. The benefit to you is that the start-up has already done a lot of what, for you, would be difficult work, so you'll have easier adaptability. They already understand the market in that country and the product they're selling—and if that product is relevant to *your* product, then you can put that understanding to good use. You can optimize it as an entry point to get into a brand-new market. Your start-up partner has already found an audience, and they are already addressing a pain point, but they are not yet big enough to do anything else by themselves.

That is where you come in: you can partner with them or even acquire them. (Acquisition can be an excellent entry point to get you into a new market.)

Unilever is a good example of a company using a platform to reach out and enter new markets. In September 2020, the company launched a platform called Uni-Excubator in China.

According to the industry trade journal *Women's Wear Daily*, Uni-Excubator is "a digitally driven incubator designed to collaborate with entrepreneurs, innovators and technology start-ups in China."[4] The idea is "to create a digitally driven incubator for China-based entrepreneurs, innovators and technology start-ups, aimed at helping Unilever bring ideas to market and launch new brands in a fraction of the time it would usually take."[5]

Uni-Excubator is an AI-based platform that shares Unilever's capabilities—their insights, information about the technologies they use, products, factories, distribution networks, and so on—with start-up entrepreneurs. The purpose of this is to drive innovation and growth for Unilever using a digital ecosystem to promote development of Unilever's brand.

Customizing Your Messaging

When you go into another country, you need to stay grounded in the values from which your brand derives its power and authority—that is, your core message. But you also need to adjust your messaging and strategy by connecting with local culture in a meaningful way.

Empathy plays a huge role in marketing and successful messaging. Wherever you go—whether to Europe or China or India or Brazil—your strategies are going to have to be adapted to the local culture, economy, and infrastructure. And the first step in doing that is to get someone on board who is native to the region and can help you understand that culture: What are their belief systems? How do they like to digest information? What kind of customer journey do they like?

Because every country is unique, every population's customer journey is unique. So the touchpoints in China, India, and the United States are all going to be different. Having local help will give you the flexibility to tailor your existing products or services to your customers' needs.

Building a Movement

The Indian business and spiritual leader Sadhguru, founder of the Isha Foundation, said that the key to entering new markets is to find an entry point and to build an organism, not an organization. An organization is kind of an abstraction, but it can also be viewed a living thing, responsive to the conditions of its environment.[6]

If you go charging into a new market and focus on nothing but fast ROI, you'll fall on your face. You need to create a *movement*. If you focus solely on how quickly you can get a return on your investment because you spent a lot of money on a few ad campaigns, then you are going to last for only a little while—and then some local competitor will come along and do the same thing you're doing and will steal your business.

Instead, you want to go in there to build a movement, a lasting impression for your brand, so that consumers will remember you and will always be drawn to you, no matter what.

Sadhguru is well-known all over the world for the same reason Unilever is well-known all over the world—because they've created movements. Companies such as Unilever have branches all over the world because they are not just selling products and services—they are connecting and engaging with their customers. They are creating a movement that aligns with their customers' belief systems and addresses their pain points and *continues* to address them as time goes on and those pain points change.

TECHNOLOGY

Tech plays a huge role in leveraging marketing strategies and creating touchpoints with customers. It is therefore important to make sure we have fresh, relevant insight on what kinds of technology the locals use and how they tend to use it.

In 2010, an India-based American entrepreneur named Valerie Wagoner made good use of that kind of insight and founded a company called ZipDial.[7]

Wagoner's company is a "missed call" marketing platform, a phenomenon mostly unknown in the United States but widely used in India and elsewhere in the developing world. Although most Indians have mobile phones, only one in three has a data connection,[8] and those who do have such connections tend to have inadequate data plans.

Wagoner noticed that Indians often send one another simple messages by calling, letting the phone ring once or twice, and then hanging up, thereby avoiding a charge for the call. The person on the receiving end of the call understands it to be a previously agreed-on message, such as "I'm on my way" or "I got home safely."

It occurred to Wagoner that this behavior could be harnessed as a way for businesses to reach people with marketing messages. ZipDial assigns each client company its own special phone number, which is used in billboard, print, and TV advertising. People call that number and hang up (thereby avoiding a charge), and the company calls or texts them back with information and a marketing message or maybe some coupons. People can also use this system to enter contests or even to place orders. This service helps ZipDial's clients— including notable organizations such as Disney, Gillette, and Greenpeace—get into underserved markets they weren't able to reach before, especially in rural areas.

To understand the huge impact of this marketing platform, it helps to also understand that the rural parts of India account for over 12 percent of the world's population. ZipDial is a perfect illustration of what I've been talking about in this chapter: Valerie Wagoner observed local customs and behavior in India, identified an entry point, and five years later, in 2015, Twitter acquired ZipDial for $30 million.[9]

INDIA CASE STUDIES

I've focused quite a bit on India in this chapter for a number of reasons. Working there is one of my many experiences. But I've also focused on India because the country is widely considered a hub of innovation, thanks in part to their enormous, diverse, dynamic population. Innovation drives growth and profits.

In my work there, I've learned that managers in India tend to be much more innovative than many of the managers I've worked with in the West. They're unafraid to take risks. They understand that it's their responsibility to dive deep into customers' issues and to keep the customer top of mind every day.

They also prioritize the well-being of their employees by building rapport and better relationships among team members, and they make a point of celebrating those people's successes. This promotes a corporate culture of unity and empowerment, which keeps everyone motivated, engaged, and focused on the company's goals.

Indian managers tend to be very concerned about making sure they have the latest market intelligence. The biggest companies in India are constantly watching start-ups to see which ones may turn out to be worth forming incubation relationships with. They know how to identify an entry point and how to envision what the success of that incubated start-up will look like.

So that you can see some of the lessons of this chapter in action, I want to share with you two assignments that I've worked on for companies in India that had a global presence. One of these clients was a global pharmaceutical company and the other was a technology company, but they were pretty similar projects—in both cases, my job was basically to conduct a cultural assessment of their different departments and divisions. The problem was they had silos within those divisions that prevented them from communicating effectively.

The other objective in both cases was to formulate effective marketing campaigns for both companies.

Our focus was on their top sales and marketing units, which were in the United States, Asia (specifically Singapore and China), and Europe. In each of these assignments, I found common themes in the problems they were struggling with.

One of the primary problems was siloing: one division wanted to outperform the other division, and they put enormous resources into their local market without bothering to try to understand the cultural differences. Also, they were not developing specific, brand-defined frameworks to address their markets, and they were not flexible or adaptive.

Part of the problem was that both of these companies needed to update their technology and out-of-date software in order to better share knowledge and data. More important than that, however, in terms of correcting the silo behavior, was to change their mindsets and get them to embrace their local partners.

We also found that the units in Asia were more innovative and delivered higher ROI than those located elsewhere. Why was that? What were they doing so differently from the rest of the organization?

First, the manager in charge of the unit in India was not only a local but also used hyperlocal insights to inform his decision-making. Moreover, he brought empathy and unity to his messaging; he brought his people together. We also noted that the managers in China used local talent, rather than in-house talent from the United States, to develop their marketing plans.

Most important, we found that the divisions that were struggling with their respective markets were more focused on ROI to the point that they were not even really connecting with their local markets. They were simply reusing plans they'd used in another market someplace else and tweaking them a bit for the local audience—and that wasn't working.

The successful managers succeeded because they relentlessly tested their marketing plans for cultural sensitivity until they were confident that they fully understood the local markets. They performed endless tests and iterations on their marketing strategies before actually implementing them—in most cases they ran a minimum of four to five iterations.

We recommended to both companies that they reengineer their brand cultures to adapt to local markets while maintaining their core values. When you go to a new market, you take your core values with you, but you can't do everything exactly the way you would in your home country. You have to learn how the local market thinks and adapt to that. Understanding the local perspective is critical to developing your market plan and strategy.

We also showcased key ways for them to connect better with how local consumers use digital platforms and recommended they adapt to local culture by understanding the local language, the types of devices people favor, and the kinds of content they tend to like. Each division and unit, we said, should have the flexibility to develop its own plan for the local market. We noticed that the divisions in Asia, which had been more successful than their colleagues elsewhere, were given more freedom by their senior managers to take risks and take deep dives into their markets in order to understand them. The other divisions didn't have that kind of freedom, and that constraint inhibited their performance.

* * *

The primary lesson to be taken from these companies' experiences is that when you are thinking about global expansion, you need to gather your insights from local observations, not from paid market research because there is a huge difference.

Finally, it bears mentioning that all the Asian and Indian managers who did so much better than their colleagues were focusing on creating some type of movement. Their work was structured by purpose and engagement, not ROI.

Local insights make your company more adaptable to enter new markets. This gives you valuable data and learning experience from experimenting and iterating. So even if the market doesn't work out for you and you fail during experimentation phases, you'll still have gained valuable knowledge that you can take with you. Without this knowledge, you will waste your time. You don't want execution failures.

In fact, experimentation is valuable before you embark on *any* new project. In science, we call it writing a hypothesis: "If X doesn't happen within Y amount of time or by spending Z amount of dollars, then we are going to iterate and make whatever changes we need to make based on that information."

When you do this, you are collecting data, setting yourself up for feedback that says, "It is working" or "It is not working." Then, if necessary, you use that data to refresh your goals and make sure you're moving in the right direction. If the data comes back negative, then you need a new goal. Use what you've learned to develop your approach to your projects and ask yourself if the approach was linear or based on circumstances. This will make your thinking and decision-making more flexible.

Business leaders should think big and practice testing out ideas on a smaller scale. Over time, this combination of mindsets helps you achieve greater success.

WHEN TO PULL THE PLUG

Succeeding in a new market requires an investment of time, money, and other resources, with no guarantee of success. So how long do you give it? What portion of your resources do you devote to a foreign market, and when is it time to say, "This isn't working" and pull the plug? And if it looks like that time has come, how do you know you're not pulling the plug prematurely?

One thing that can be extended during your development phase is your incubation period. Here you can monitor your attempts to sell your product or services following a launch. Focus on supply and demand: Are there any restrictions? What are they, and can the company overcome them?

Write a hypothesis. In science, this is done to help us make precise predictions based on prior research. In business, writing hypotheses can keep you focused and help you define and direct your research further.

There is no data that says your incubation period in a new market should last X amount of time; therefore, it's important to prototype, collect data via testing, show it to customers, retest, validate the data, and then move forward. This can be repeated as many times as necessary until you gather enough validation data to move forward. Best Buy failed to open new stores in the United Kingdom because British customers did not like "big box" stores, and Starbucks failed to open in Australia because customers there preferred local coffee shops over chains. The most important thing is to learn from the data so you can use it somewhere else.[10]

* * *

The success of your market expansion depends on how hard you work and how strong your organization is. If you are a company that has a lot of silos, if your financials are not good, if your culture is not innovative, if your employees don't have the necessary motivation and are not all on the same page, then an international venture is going to be difficult because there will likely never be synergy among the different branches.

Everything depends on the organization—and on the aspirations of the people *within* the organization and whether those aspirations are tied to the organization's purpose. Consider Samsung: their purpose is to "devote talent and technology to creating superior products," which is why they invest in their employees.

If your aspirations are too high and you don't have the right kinds of capabilities to achieve them, then you will not succeed. If, on the other hand, you have tremendous talent and capability but you are not reaching high enough, then you will have wasted all that potential.

Either way, the choice is yours.

KEY TAKEAWAYS

- One of the best ways to ensure that your company is prepared to deal with unexpected external events is to expand into new markets whenever possible.

- Try your neighboring state or a neighboring city before you try expanding nationally.

- When entering any new market, engage local partners who can provide local insight.

5

FINDING NEW CHANNELS AND INCREASING EFFICIENCY

Business has only two basic functions: marketing and innovation.

—PETER DRUCKER[1]

IN THIS CHAPTER I'd like to talk about finding new channels, going to market faster and smarter, and partnering with others to get the word out in new ways.

Effective messaging (how you reach your customers) is one of the most important concerns any business has. The best way to achieve this end is to develop multiple channels to connect with the public and to use messaging designed to appeal to the people who are most likely to need your product or service.

It's important to think creatively. Every CEO and business owner understands the importance of innovation (indeed, countless books have been written on that topic), but there's more to innovation than creating new products. Finding new messaging and distribution channels to improve customer engagement is also a vital form of innovation, one that will pay dividends by enabling you to go to market faster with new product offerings.

The first step toward developing a faster and more efficient channel is to identify how your customers—both existing and potential—actually consume the product messaging that reaches them. It is important to scrutinize all aspects of your current operations and distribution channels so you can identify any untapped opportunities that may exist.

Look at Apple and Microsoft: What do they do that makes their product launches so successful so quickly? What kinds of channels do they use to get to market faster?

When Apple launched the iPhone, their marketing channels comprised both physical and online settings, and those channels drove sales not just of the iPhone but also Apple's many other products. In the physical realm (i.e., within the brick-and-mortar Apple stores), they have their support center, the famous "Genius Bar." This serves multiple purposes: First, it provides iPhone users with a way to get in-person, face-to-face help when something goes wrong with their phones. This reinforces Apple's brand and fosters customer loyalty—a customer experience effect that is bolstered by the aesthetic design of the store itself. Second, it puts the customer in an environment where he or she can see—and buy—all of Apple's other products.

Apple thinks of everything when they launch a new product, and that is why they get to the market so quickly.

Similarly, when Microsoft launched Windows 95, they opened product support centers—accessible online and by telephone—in advance. Before the new operating system was even launched, Microsoft was prepared to ensure that their customers would have all the support they needed to get up and running as quickly as possible. Like Apple's Genius Bar, these support centers enabled them to get to market quickly; they sold over a million copies of the software in just four days and seven million within the first five weeks.[2]

But what if your company lacks the deep pockets, broad product offerings, and bottomless resources that make Apple and Microsoft the behemoths they are? Not to worry. Numerous marketing and distribution channels are available to you that don't cost hundreds of millions of dollars. In this chapter, we will explore three of those options: forming partnerships, direct-to-consumer distribution strategies, and multichannel campaigns.

FORMING PARTNERSHIPS

Exploring mutually beneficial partnerships will benefit not only you and your partners but also your customers. For an example of what can be accomplished in this way, let's look at CNETT, the Caribbean Network for Empowerment Through Training.

CNETT uses a subscription model to support the development of small businesses and microbusinesses in the Caribbean by offering personal coaching and business innovation programs. They have partnered with Mindvalley, a Malaysia-based online personal growth platform, and with Humanity's Team, a global transformation education program based in Colorado, to expand their product and service offerings. Thanks to this partnership, CNETT is able to explore opportunities they would not be able to find on their own and to meet customer demands that fall outside their area of expertise. These partnerships provide a broader reach of prospective customers: CNETT can offer Mindvalley's products and services separately or consolidate them with their own offerings—and all three companies can utilize one another's marketing platforms and thereby reach a broader audience.

When looking for partners, how do you decide who would be an appropriate match? CNETT looked for partners that aligned with their purpose and had a consciousness-oriented business model like their own. Your criteria will most likely differ from theirs, but in general, you should seek out businesses whose offerings overlap slightly (but not completely!) with your own. What you're looking for is synergy.

DIRECT-TO-CONSUMER DISTRIBUTION STRATEGIES

Let's look at a medical device company called Eargo, which

makes hearing aids—and goes to market faster by employing an unorthodox distribution channel.

As of 2019 there are forty-three million US adults with hearing loss, only 27 percent of whom own a hearing aid. The three main factors driving this disparity are cost, accessibility, and stigma.

The hearing aid industry overwhelmingly requires consumers to pay out of pocket, as most people's health plans offer very limited insurance coverage for these devices—or no insurance coverage at all. And most hearing aids are costly—they often run in excess of $4,000. This cost exacerbates the accessibility issue; one generally has to go to a hearing loss clinic or an audiologist to get a hearing aid. Finally, a stigma is attached to them: most hearing aids are ugly, conspicuous medical devices traditionally associated with the elderly—and nobody wants to look old.

Taken together, these facts indicate that before Eargo came along, there was an unpenetrated market to be served. Eargo addressed these issues by creating a nearly invisible product that sits *inside* the ear rather than behind it, where everyone can see it. (The device looks a bit like Apple AirPods.) The product also uses Bluetooth-enabled technology that allows it to be paired with a mobile phone, and it comes with a charging case. Best of all, Eargo's hearing aid products are typically half the cost of their competitors' wares.

But the thing that most differentiates Eargo from their competitors is their business model: Other hearing aid companies sell their products to hearing loss clinics that mark up the price before selling them to consumers. Eargo, on the other hand, is a direct-to-consumer provider, much like Warby Parker, which sells trendy prescription glasses directly online— and sells them a lot cheaper than you can get them from an optometrist. Warby Parker basically eliminated the middleman so now you don't have to go to an eye care provider to get glasses. You can buy them online and get them delivered to your home.

Eargo uses essentially that same business model to reach their customers. They also offer unlimited lifetime telemedicine support in the form of phone consults with audiologists— indeed, they form *partnerships* with their audiologists.

Eargo arrived at this business model by analyzing three basic things: their competitors' offerings (i.e., their products and how they sold them to the clinics), their customers' needs (they understood the stigma, cost, and limited access problems), and their own capabilities (their invisible in-the-ear design, advanced technology, and the telecare available from their audiologist partners). These three components provided a differentiating factor for Eargo to go to market faster.

Because Eargo knows that their competitors' offers may improve or their customers' needs may change, they are constantly innovating while continuously collecting data from their current customers: What do they want? How do they want it? How can we improve the product so it works better for them? They also form partnerships with insurance companies, audiologists, and other companies that can help them spread the word about Eargo.

Eargo has developed a distribution model that differentiates them by taking a complex process and making it cheaper and more convenient for the customer. The company has built up both online and traditional channels to build efficient multi-channel customer acquisition.

More important, however, Eargo linked their remarkable product innovation—an almost invisible product that sits inside the ear—to a distribution strategy that allowed them to go to market faster.

Linking product innovation and strategy is the key here: combining what makes you unique—your value proposition— with how are you delivering it differently from your competitors. Aligning these two things, innovation and strategy, is what allows you to get to market faster. Companies that don't have that alignment between what they are offering and how they are going to do it will tend to struggle.

USING DIGITAL *AND* TRADITIONAL CHANNELS

I want to talk about a work assignment I had where we used a multichannel approach to drive faster market reach. A while back, a major leading skincare player asked me to develop a competitive, winning strategy to help it cope with disruption in its market space.

The company had noticed a significant drop (10 percent!) in revenue as its customers began to drift toward the trendy natural and organic products offered by smaller and newer competitors. In response to these market signals, the company had reformulated its product, and our team now faced the challenge of launching this reformulated product into the fiercely competitive organic and natural market.

This wasn't going to be easy: our main competitor in the leading skincare category was able to boast that it was the number-one skincare-recommended brand. We couldn't make that kind of claim, so in order to build a competitive strategy, we had to make sure that we were able to reach our audience faster than the other company could.

To properly understand the market trends, we needed to understand our customers' journey—how they were consuming the information that led them to their product choices. How could we compete with our rivals? How could we draw the attention of the millennial consumers we were targeting toward our established brand—and away from these fancy new organic brands? What is the fastest and best way to reach them? How do these customers like to consume information? How do you break through the noise from other brands that are already marketing on the same channels as you are?

We knew that our target audience, millennials, tends to search for information on their smartphones. We conducted independent market research and found that most searches for organic products in the skincare market were done via mobile phones. With this insight, we built an aggressive multichannel, multimedia campaign strategy focused primarily on mobile users.

Our marketing plan needed to stabilize brand trust and regain growth trajectory, so our messaging focused on the reformulation of our skincare product, emphasizing that it was now all-natural and organic and didn't contain any chemicals.

Our strategy was to focus on the brand's DNA to showcase its expertise in this particular type of product category.

The campaign was launched on mobile first in order to achieve a quick response from the target audience but that was quickly followed by a multimedia strategy. A mobile campaign is a digital marketing strategy that targets an audience on smartphones, tablets, and other mobile devices using SMS, social media, email, websites, and apps.

The mobile campaign produced 30 percent of our ad recall results—a huge accomplishment. It outperformed all other aspects of the multimedia strategy we had during that time. The total sales growth for this campaign was 12 percent for the brand, and the specific brand promotion grew 1.5 times faster than the total brand portfolio. The campaign worked really well, and we were able to get to market much faster than if we had just used a traditional online campaign.

Although it's common knowledge that the last twenty years have seen a large shift to consumers using digital media, brands are actually able to reach audiences much quicker and easier when they complement their digital media with traditional media. It is critical for expansion to always look for new channels. Mobile is different from an online desktop platform. A newspaper is a different platform from radio, magazines, or billboards—and all of these channels have their specific uses, depending on who your target market is. We used the mobile channel for that leading skincare brand because that was where our audience was spending the majority of its time consuming information in its search for skincare products. You want to focus on the channels where your customers spend the largest amount of their time.

MEASURING SUCCESS

It's important to be willing to experiment and take chances. CNETT didn't know for certain whether their partnerships with Mindvalley and Humanity's Team would work out—it's not a given that any other specific company is going to be the right partner for you to connect with. But when you start seeing more sales and more engagement on your website, then you know that whatever you're doing is working.

Above all, you should never stop collecting data. I recently stated that what worked last year may not work this year, and what works this year may not work in the future.[3] Data collection helps you stay on top of market trends.

How do you measure success? How can you tell whether what you're doing is working? The evidence is in your results. Microsoft knew their strategy was working when they sold seven million copies of Windows 95.

Regarding my skincare assignment, once we started developing our messaging, we started getting data right away. We saw that sales of a lotion we advertised on the mobile platform outperformed all the other products in our portfolio by 150 percent.

When you see data like that, it is telling you that your messaging is working. It is telling you that the communications strategy you used to reach the market faster than your competitor actually worked—because your sales went up. With the recent 10 percent decrease in sales, your company is now experiencing a 10 to 15 percent increase. If you see a lot of engagement in a short period of time, you will know.

Usually you can get useful data within three to six weeks. Once we started seeing quick engagement, we made sure we redoubled our focus on mobile. If we hadn't seen any engagement on mobile, we would have stopped what we were doing and tried another channel.

That is how you know what works—through testing and experimentation.

* * *

Product alone does not increase sales. A brand-new innovation is not going to guarantee increased sales or reaching your market faster. What *does* work is combining the delivery with the right channel so that you understand how your customers consume both your product and your messaging.

When you are looking at new channels or looking to reach the market faster with your products and services, your success really comes down to two things: experimentation and understanding your customer's needs. When you have that understanding, it is a starting point for you to move forward and experiment whether you're trying a new distribution model, channel, or partnership.

Is there a penalty for standing still, for not doing all of this? Yes, absolutely. If you're launching a brand-new product and you are not utilizing all your channels, a competitor is going to come along very quickly and do the same thing you're doing. And then you will no longer exist because that competitor will probably already have the resources, money, and talent—everything it needs to make the same innovative product you've just launched. And it is going to do it much faster than you will.

So you have to stay one step ahead, and the only way to do that is to utilize the right channels to reach your audience and to constantly innovate and continually improve your products and services.

It's okay to imitate the competition to find new channels and build new business models. Companies should take advantage of customer and market-trend data from other companies that have already developed new operating systems—and that's exactly what Eargo, Apple, and CNETT did in the examples presented in this chapter. They were able to develop connected experiences through their channels, which built customer loyalty through the entire life cycle of their products and services.

One advantage of this approach is that because you're copying an established process, you are able to save yourself a lot of the iterative testing that would have been necessary for a process you develop yourself.

Seek out new channel innovations to create new delivery systems, and if possible, simplify your process using platforms. Your customers will love it!

KEY TAKEAWAYS

- With industries moving from an earlier model to providing new channels using advances in technology, constant innovation investment is a necessity.

- The first step toward developing a faster and more efficient channel is to identify how your customer base prefers to consume product messaging.

- Product alone does not increase sales. What *does* work is combining the delivery with the right channel.

- Platforms are here to stay! You should find more platforms where you can promote your business and build new channels for customers.

PART II
Innovation and Collaboration

6

WHEN YOU'RE NOT INNOVATING ENOUGH—AND WHAT TO DO ABOUT IT

I believe in innovation, and that the way you get innovation is you fund research and you learn the basic facts.

—BILL GATES[1]

WHAT DOES THE WORD *innovation* mean to you?

When they hear that word, most people think of new kinds of products and services—sudden, disruptive changes to the status quo. But there are other ways to think about innovation and there are more productive, sustainable ways to innovate.

Every ten years, PricewaterhouseCoopers (PwC) publishes their "Global Innovation 1,000 Study," in which they look at a thousand companies to examine how well they innovate compared to the money they spend on R&D over a fifteen-year period.[2] PwC's most recent study, from 2018, found that high-leverage innovators—companies that outperformed others in their industry despite spending less money on R&D—had six factors in common:

1. They closely align innovation strategy with business strategy.

2. They create company-wide cultural support for innovation.

3. Their top leadership is highly involved with the innovation program.

4. They base innovation on direct insights from end users.

5. They rigorously control project selection early in the innovation process.

6. They excel at each of these first five characteristics and have been able to integrate them to create unique customer experiences that can transform their markets.

PwC's contention is that when you build these six capabilities, you have sustainable financial performance in good times *and* in bad times. It is not about how much money you spend; rather, it is about aligning your strategy, culture, and capabilities and developing a deep understanding of your customer in order to build innovation strategies.

In light of this, we should not be asking ourselves whether we should prioritize or invest in innovation. Innovation should not only be a priority for survival but also for creating new sustainable growth.

HOW TO FAIL AT INNOVATION

Remember Circuit City? If you're under the age of twenty-five or so, you probably don't—they filed for bankruptcy in 2008 and went out of business in 2009. They didn't evolve to meet their customers' changing needs, and they lacked market and customer behavior insights.

Of course, no twenty-first-century conversation about failure to innovate can fail to mention Blockbuster, which was unable (or unwilling) to transition to a digital model, even in the face of the clear threat of Netflix's business model. Like Circuit City, Blockbuster failed to evolve along with the changing market and adapt to the changing behaviors of its customers. (In fact, Blockbuster actually offered to acquire Circuit City in April 2008, only to reverse course a few months later.[3] With the benefit of hindsight, it's hard not to laugh at the optimism of this move.)

I won't dwell on this—today's business literature is rife with stories about companies that failed to innovate and evolve when the times demanded it, and Blockbuster is now a well-worn punching bag in those conversations. It's more interesting to look at companies that actually do innovate—and why those innovations sometimes fail.

No one would confuse Amazon with Blockbuster or Circuit City, but not everything Jeff Bezos touches turns to gold. As Exhibit A in support of that statement, I give you the Amazon Fire Phone.

The Fire Phone failed because Amazon overengineered the product. The hardware had too many features (e.g., five camera lenses positioned around the device for a "Dynamic Perspective" that was supposed to simulate 3D imaging) and the operating system was poorly designed; tech writer David Marin called it "a stiffer version of Android without the Google suite of apps or the Play Store."[4] Worst of all, the product was too expensive.

Amazon was so determined to become a beloved lifestyle brand like Apple and to compete with Apple on those terms that, paradoxically, they actually managed to recklessly rush an overdeveloped product into the market. Apple achieved their position by painstaking, iterative, *incremental* innovation and by building public trust in their brand over decades. When Amazon tried to leapfrog over that process, they fell flat on their face. They had to withdraw the Fire Phone from the market only a year after it was launched, and they haven't tried to make anything like it since then.

PORSCHE: THE POWER OF INNOVATION

In contrast to Amazon, let's look at a company that *successfully* tried something new. Let's look at the Cayenne, Porsche's version of an SUV.

If Porsche had tried to sell an SUV in the 1980s, they probably would have been laughed out of the market. Even today we primarily associate the Porsche name with high-performance sports cars—that's their brand. That's what they're known for. They are not known for family sedans or for the kinds of cars suburban moms use to drive their kids to soccer practice.

So before they tried to enter a new market, the company collected lots of consumer data—I mean *tons* of it—for many years. They took surveys. They held car clinics where they showed people samples of what a different kind of Porsche could look like. They invested a lot of time and resources in lengthy ideation and development phases that ultimately produced the Panamera, a four-door family sedan.

The Panamera was a success, but it was only a stepping-stone. Porsche continued to collect insights from consumers, looking into everything from whether they wanted a larger cup holder to whether an SUV should have extra room in the trunk. Any SUV they built had to have Porsche DNA—the sleek look, the engine design, and so on.

At the same time, they had to keep brand considerations in mind: they had to address consumer concerns about Porsche building an SUV in the first place—a significant part of their audience didn't even want them to make the SUV because they thought it wouldn't be right, that it wouldn't align with who they are. Porsche management used their car clinics to try to convert that segment of the market, getting consumers' feedback and planting seeds in their minds—*what-if?*

The Cayenne was launched in 2002, and today it is the best-selling vehicle in Porsche's portfolio. This success was no accident—Porsche did everything right: They were patient. They collected data. They iterated. They tested their ideas, and then they brought the product to the market. And today they are no longer just a sports car company; by collecting practical insights, they were able to create a new market demand that their company could address.

The takeaway is that companies that do well and maintain stability, even during turbulent times, are the ones that focus on radical innovation with a long-term vision. Magnus Penker and Dr. S. B. Khoh demonstrated in a 2018 publication that radical innovators also are stronger in incremental innovation; that is, they are better at both improving existing concepts and developing new ones. The radical component strengthens both.[5]

Focusing on radical innovations enables companies to stay ahead of competitors by anticipating what customers will want next. When you're uncertain how you should proceed with a new project or how you should target audiences going forward, collecting insights from close observations of how your product is used helps point you in the right direction.

CULTURE AND CAPABILITY

Incremental innovation is a continuous process, and it requires discipline and clear focus. It needs to be supported by an aligned culture that has an innovative mindset and by capabilities that differentiate the company from its competitors.

Culture is important: if your organizational culture is focused on profit and product first, then you're in big trouble. If your culture is not consumer driven and your leaders are not equipped with the necessary end-user insights to drive market growth, then you're cooking with a recipe for failure. Because Blockbuster and Circuit City were monomaniacally focused on their products and their profits, they didn't understand what their customers wanted or that consumer desires were evolving. If your culture is focused on customers first, as Porsche's culture is, then it can drive incremental innovation—and growth—for your company.

The cultural challenges that we see in our work vary from company to company, but a common thread is that the people within a company's culture don't know the company's purpose and can't identify its value proposition. The leaders of these companies don't communicate purpose clearly enough, and more important, it's not reinforced; their communications lack conviction.

Another challenge we see is that strategy and execution are not disciplined, so leaders end up launching ad hoc initiatives based on very little data.

Speaking to a journalist about his mentor, Audrey MacLean, Netflix CEO Reed Hastings said, "From her I learned the value of focus. I learned it is better to do one product well than two products in a mediocre way."[6] In order to grow and innovate, companies have to be laser focused. They have to align their capabilities, and there has to be harmony between their strategy and execution. It's a domino effect: The benefit of having a clear vision and value proposition is that your decisions will be clear in turn—and then your strategy will be crystal clear. That clear strategy increases your success rate and reduces your R&D cost because you are not fishing around and grabbing at ideas that don't align with who you are or what your capabilities are (more on capabilities in a moment). Your resources are then directed toward whichever initiatives promise the highest return.

* * *

Now let's define the word *capability*. Capability is a combination of processes, tools, knowledge, and skills that differentiates a company in the market—for example, a company's ability to use claim-based marketing for a pediatric skincare product. Or they may have a lean and flexible manufacturing process, or the sales team may have a fantastic relationship with its key customers. A capability could even be something as simple as a highly efficient inventory system. (This is Walmart's key differentiator, and it is a very strong capability for them.)

When strong capabilities come together, they make you flexible and enable you to adapt quickly in your markets, which gives you a game-day competitive advantage. Your capabilities are the core strengths of your company, and it is important to preserve them.

* * *

I want to tell you about a work assignment in which I addressed cultural gaps and misalignment for a global company that makes commercial appliance products.

We started with a vigorous data-collection process. First, we conducted a lot of interviews with employees and found that this company had trouble sharing information and best practices across the organization. The teams were not motivated and they had siloed business units. Critically, we found that decision-making authority and accountability were not aligned and that the company lacked customer insight when developing its strategy.

Using a proven methodology and framework, we addressed these challenges by first creating alignment across the division through improving communication of the company's goals. Second, we identified which capabilities it should focus on strengthening—in particular, understanding customer behavior and acquiring insight into the user experience.

Third, we focused on aligning its strategies by improving its ability to clearly communicate the company's vision. In our experience, communication problems in a company often come down to a language problem: groups within an organization have their own set of jargon and codes that they use. What's needed, therefore, is a common language, a common frame of reference for everyone.

Lastly, the company needed to build a culture of learning,

purpose, and alignment. Building a culture with a specific mindset is important because that mindset will determine what your company is capable of doing in the market. Team members are naturally influenced by one another, and that influence creates a domino effect of positive or negative habits and behaviors.

We also identified behaviors that were inhibiting innovation. We asked the team to rate the following statement from a scale of 1 to 5: "Leaders at all levels enable me to take ownership of my work and help me remove obstacles that come up." When your managers and directors don't have the necessary support and coaching, or even the resources they need, it becomes difficult for them to produce results. It's important to connect your teams' work to a purpose and a culture that supports the business strategy and the operations. These things are all linked. Leaders are responsible for igniting that spark, which fosters the commitment and passion necessary to support the work that needs to be done. In some cases what appears at first to be a strategy problem turns out to be a culture problem instead; the strategies are not working because the employees don't have a clear vision of where they are going and thus aren't committed or passionate about what they are doing.

We checked in with this organization a year later, and I'm happy to say that after implementing our recommendations, the company launched a new service with 100 percent success, and it has reduced its lead time to the market by 25 percent by aligning its vision and strategies.

* * *

Bank of America (BoA) is a great example of a culture-focused company. The financial industry is not generally an innovative one, but BoA has been around for a very long time, and they know what they're doing. Their chief client care executive once said he believes that the more you invest in your employees, the better the services for their customers. "We've got to pay attention to every single one of these 10 billion interactions," he said, "and get every single interaction right."

Think for a minute—why would he say this? Why is it that important that every interaction counts? Because customer service is everything to them. Because BoA is one of the largest companies in the world, and they want to stay that way.

BoA also understands that in order to stay competitive, investing in employees is crucial, so they are heavily invested in their employees. They provide academy training that focuses on creating value and optimal user experience for their customers. They are also great at offering incentives and sharing wins and losses with their teams. They engage with their employees by providing coaching and leadership support and by communicating clear goals.

In 2020, amid a stalled economy and unstable interest rates, BoA's consumer loans actually increased, and they experienced overall growth in all of their business units.[7] How does a company maintain growth during a recession? What is their secret?

They have strong capabilities: They have the necessary

resources and relevant customer insights to continue providing new products and services as planned. They have a strong, engaging culture, and they have alignment across their business segment. Such companies are always able to continue work as usual in the face of unexpected events such as a pandemic or a recession.

DISCIPLINE

I've mentioned the importance of discipline a couple of times in this chapter, but what does it mean for a company to be disciplined?

In the work we do, we create a framework, a step-by-step process to go to market. And once that framework has been established, it is done the same way each and every time.

For example, if you are launching a new product, you're not just looking at ideas and guessing which ones are going to work or which idea is going to resonate with the market. Through a meticulous ideation process, you align *every* idea with your core capabilities and your purpose. Like a scientist, you start with hypotheses—when we take an idea to the market, this is what should happen. If the idea doesn't work, then we're going to iterate that idea; we're going to iterate the hypothesis based on the new data we collected while going through the development phase—as Porsche did.

Porsche knew they couldn't just go from a two-door sedan to an SUV; it would have been off-brand, and it just wouldn't have worked. They couldn't just go from that point A to point B without making sure that point B aligned with who they are, with their DNA. They are a sports car company, and they know they can't jump that far in one shot, so they need to take steps. That's why they made a four-door family sedan first.

When you write hypotheses, they will help bridge gaps in your research by giving you time for reflection while you're collecting new data points or ideas from other sources. It also helps give you a heads-up if an idea that was initially thought to be worth pursuing may not have merit after all. One way that companies such as Porsche and Apple produce amazingly successful products is through continuous feedback loops, which are further supported by hypotheses about where customers want their products to go next in order to maximize customer satisfaction with each iteration. Yet most businesses don't take advantage of this framework because they're too afraid of failure to focus on building successes.

This is one of the disciplines we teach in our framework.

SHOOTING FOR THE MOON

In their book *Built to Last: Successful Habits of Visionary Companies*, authors Jim Collins and Jerry I. Porras extol the virtues of Big, Hairy, Audacious Goals (BHAGs).[8] Everyone wants a disruptive BHAG. Everyone wants to shoot for the moon and create something that is totally new—but a disciplined process of testing and experimentation needs to come first.

Transformative goals are great, and they get everybody excited, but they are not enough. If you do manage to achieve them, it is because you took the time along the way to create a disciplined culture of constant innovation. It's important to create alignment of your goals and your capabilities and a disciplined culture toward ongoing incremental innovation. If you do not have strong capabilities and a disciplined culture that is oriented toward ongoing innovation, those big goals are going to be for naught.

The goal of any company should not be to grow profit just for the sake of growing profit. Big goals, even if they seem unrealistic at first glance, can create a culture that is dynamic and full of energy. The lack thereof leads to an uninspired atmosphere with no real direction or excitement, which ultimately has negative consequences for the business. In fact, I often see companies where the *lack* of a moonshot goal is the problem. The leaders of these companies ask us, "Why is the culture not aligned? Why are there siloed business units and departments?" The reason is that there is no cohesion, no higher purpose, and no clarity.

Everything comes back to purpose, clarity, and vision. If you don't have that clarity in the beginning, when the company is growing, or if you lose that vision along the way, then the company may grow really big—but you'll find that you now have misaligned cultures and endemic bad habits. When you don't have clarity, your team will be less motivated, less engaged. Without that engagement, they are not going to come together as a workforce.

The companies that successfully shoot for the moon are ones that practice not only incremental innovation but also radical innovation (and simultaneously looking at long-term success). Innovation begins with experimentation, the by-product of data collection and experimenting with bold new ideas to pursue moonshot goals. Those audacious goals become achievable when you get the hang of experimenting, failing, and repeating. Use your purpose to drive bold new visions and practice experimentation to increase your flexibility and adaptability as Porsche and Apple did.

KEY TAKEAWAYS

- Innovation is not only a matter of survival but also necessary for sustainable growth.

- Focusing on radical innovation enables companies to stay ahead of competitors by anticipating what customers will want next.

- Innovations are a natural outgrowth of experimentation and iteration.

- Bigger goals can create a culture that's dynamic and full of energy.

7

STALK YOUR CUSTOMERS:

Obtaining Customer Insights

Your most unhappy customers are your greatest source of learning.

—**BILL GATES**[1]

WHAT ARE THEY THINKING?

That's what companies ask about their buyers (or, more accurately, about the people who *aren't* buying!) every day. But instead of trying to get real answers to that question, they guess, make stuff up, or just throw up their hands and declare that customers are too irrational to understand.

Here's a novel thought: ask them.

Ask your current, past, and potential customers what they think and let those observations lead to the insights that spark flashes of marketing genius.

Without insight, a company has no way to spot the hidden dangers of hard-to-read market trends. Without insight, you never know when a competitor may be positioning itself to eat your lunch. Without insight, you're always vulnerable to unexpected external events—if you don't follow weather reports, you'll never know when a tornado may be poised to drop out of the sky and demolish your house.

In this chapter we'll explore the opportunities that present themselves when you build and nurture an authentic, meaningful connection with your customers, and we'll look at the best ways to ensure that you always have up-to-date, relevant insight into their needs and desires.

OBSERVATIONS

Let me tell you about an observation I made that helped a pharmaceutical company improve its sales practices and thereby improve its relationships with its customer base.

The company was concerned that its sales material wasn't producing much engagement, so I asked if I could accompany a sales rep to one of his meetings with a doctor, just to see how he did things.

I went to a hospital with the sales rep and watched him interact with the doctor. The rep gave his presentation covering the benefits of the drug we were marketing, how it compared with other drugs on the market, and so on. Observing from a distance, I watched his iPad slideshow and listened to the Q&A session that followed. I noticed that while the rep was cheerfully flying through his slide deck, the doctor looked a little confused. He didn't seem to understand the benefits of the drug, and he certainly didn't see its advantages over another drug the hospital was already using. He also seemed a little bit "checked out," a bit impatient; I caught him checking his watch a lot.

Why is he so uncomfortable? I wondered. Was something about the sales rep's pitch not clear? Or was the doctor in a hurry to go somewhere? Was the presentation a little too long?

There was very little engagement from this doctor during that meeting. When we were leaving, we found out that the meeting had been scheduled during his lunch hour.

We spoke to quite a few doctors that day, and I noticed a common theme in those conversations: the doctors all seemed irritated and frustrated, unable to understand (or too impatient to understand) some of what we were showing them.

From this firsthand observation we were able to spot some key things that we could do differently in the future: We could improve our slides, presenting the information in smaller, bite-size chunks to convey our message more succinctly. It would also be better, we realized, not to schedule meetings with the doctors during their lunchtime when it's harder for them even to focus on the conversation. Better to meet first thing in the morning, when they're a bit fresher, or later in the afternoon, when most of that day's crises have been dealt with.

Finally, acting on mistaken assumptions, we clearly hadn't done a very good job explaining the benefits of our drug compared to a competitor's product—our sales reps' presentations needed improvement. We learned that we should always test the detail aid in its "natural environment" (the fifteen-minute interaction between the rep and the health-care provider), and we should co-create the content between sales and marketing in order to obtain buy-in. Adopting a fail-fast mindset, we were able to update and improve the detail aid.

INSIGHTS

Now let's talk about insight. An insight is one step beyond an observation. An insight, by definition, is a profound and useful understanding of a person, a thing, a situation, or an issue. Insights help to join data points and provide evidence based on certainty. An insight can help us innovate and find new and different ways to do things, which in turn helps us improve our products and services.

For an example of how data collection leads to insight, we can look at Proctor & Gamble (P&G), maker of Febreze. P&G saw a drop in Febreze sales in Japan, so they sent researchers to the homes of the Japanese housewives who used the product. They noticed that these women were using the product differently than American consumers did, spraying it on their mattress, their living room curtains, and their sofas—which is not how Febreze was designed to be used. As originally conceived, it was intended to mask odors in closets full of sneakers and things like that. When the researchers asked, "Why are you doing this?" the women responded, "Well, we can't wash these things, but we really want them to smell good and we want to feel that they are clean, so we use Febreze instead."

Based on this feedback, the P&G researchers came up with an insight: Febreze can be considered for different kinds of household uses. This insight inspired a new campaign, *I Wish I Could Wash*, which drove a substantial increase in sales in Japan. Following that success, P&G deployed this campaign globally, increasing Febreze sales everywhere else in the world. By actually going into homes where their product was being used, they were better able to understand the consumer. That's the power of insight.

Another P&G insight led to an improvement of Cascade dishwashing liquid. P&G's research found that most moms didn't fully trust their dishwashers, so they prewashed their dishes before putting them into the dishwasher. This insight inspired a new product called Cascade Platinum, a stronger liquid that enables the user to "skip the pre-wash and say goodbye to tough, burnt-on messes and 24-hour stuck-on food."[2] P&G created an ad campaign that emphasized the time and effort busy moms could save, and by doing this they were able to increase sales *and* help their customers use their product more effectively.

* * *

The best way to approach insights is to gather as much data as possible. Then, when that data has produced an insight, it is very important to test it rather than just run with it. To illustrate this, I want to tell you about an assignment I had to collect data and obtain insights for an over-the-counter (OTC) nonprescription pain medicine brand.

Based on a market research report, the pharma company was concerned that some people weren't using its product properly and that this misuse was creating a widespread safety problem. Our goal was to drive awareness of proper, safe use of OTC NSAIDs (over-the-counter nonsteroidal anti-inflammatory drugs) and to change consumer behavior.

We conducted a behavior study using video cameras to monitor how our test subjects lived over a period of a few weeks, and we watched how they took their OTC medicines. Our study revealed specific misuse patterns among certain segments of the population. We found that these patterns were associated with specific types of people and that the patterns were related to very specific underlying attitudes.

One segment's attitude could best be summed up as "I know my body, and therefore I know what my body can handle—so you don't need to tell me what dosage I should be taking, because *I know* what is best for *me*." Another segment had such busy lifestyles that they would just automatically and immediately reach for an OTC medicine for stress relief or to prevent headaches rather than treat them.

Our team focused on increasing knowledge about appropriate use via different channel and messaging strategies. The focus was that we wanted our consumers to use our product *safely*. We invited all the involved stakeholders—retail teams, science teams, marketing teams, efficacy groups, and others—to participate in an ideation workshop to help create the right type of messaging for behavior change: how could we best connect with our consumers?

We devised a focus strategy that aligned with our core brand message—to provide safe products to our customers—and we formulated a proactive communication strategy to educate the public on safe over-the-counter use of NSAIDs. We used behavioral science and an anthropological approach to understand and change dangerous behavior, such as not reading direction labels or combining OTC NSAIDs with other medicines, which can lead to bad reactions or overdoses.

We ended up creating twenty-five different pieces of educational content, and we reinforced the brand's commitment to public health. Our efforts drove a 90 percent behavior change to appropriate use and a 76 percent increase in awareness of the dangers of combining OTC medicines, and we formed twenty external partnerships to address public misuse of OTC medicines.

As a result of all this effort, we aligned our capabilities with our core message to the customer—basically, we let them know we want them to use our products safely, and if they don't, these are the bad things that can happen.

ANTHROPOLOGY AND DATA

As companies grow, they become more complex, and this puts pressure on the organization to gain accurate customer insights. This pressure prompts business leaders to turn to big data for information about markets, but quantitative data cannot explain *why* customers make the decisions they make.

Companies need to combine big data and an anthropological approach to address gaps that can be difficult to identify without seeing consumers conducting tasks in context. An anthropological approach is where teams with an anthropologist's background are responsible for contributing research-based insights that frame and inspire ideas. During their research to solve a problem, they may stumble across new ways to frame issues and uncover insights leading to novel solutions. The observations made by the P&G teams, the pharma sales rep tour, and the OTC team lacked any hypotheses about what they might find.

These examples enabled business leaders to go beyond research findings, which are driven by an overreliance on conscious, rational, and explicit memories. The anthropology approach examines the root of the decision-making process, which is often subconscious, implicit, and emotionally driven. This nonlinear process creates motivations that inform consumer behavior, which can lead to insights that enable transformations in product development and services.

MARKET TRENDS

Anthropologists aren't the only ones who study cultures and reach conclusions. So do marketers! Don't collect data just to look at it today and quickly rush a new project or a service out into the market for an easy, short-term ROI. Look at market trends. What are the market trends saying, and how can you use that data to anticipate the future? Understanding market trends helps you understand where the market is going and the kind of data you should be collecting in the first place.

The global fintech (financial technology) industry is growing fast, with a focus on mobile devices. In 2020, the number of banking and fintech apps grew by 20.3 percent. This development reflects a huge rise in start-ups that are developing technology to enable the financial sector to provide more seamless services.

Many global banks see this as an opportunity and not a threat. Banks are paying attention to these trends, and many of them are starting to offer mobile banking if they haven't already done so. Goldman Sachs estimates that in the next few years up to $4.7 trillion in revenue will migrate from banks to new companies in the fintech sector, with 33 percent of millennials believing they will not need banks in the future.

Given these predictions, what is the banking industry doing now to ensure they stay relevant in the future? Do banks really have an opportunity to expand to more segments under these market circumstances? Can a bank successfully target college students to get them to open their first bank accounts?

HSBC seems to think so. This global bank led a student-focused social media campaign in the United Kingdom, and over a one-year period they achieved an astonishing *747 percent* increase in student account sign-ups from that campaign. I have run a lot of marketing campaigns, and I'm here to tell you that 747 percent is just mind-blowing.

HSBC targeted students because they have the potential to become lifetime customers—but how did they do it?

The bank's research found that one of the best predictors of a successful future for students is having a diverse social network. That was the first insight. Taking this insight further, they moved to build an emotional connection with those students via social media.

Their other research-driven insight: the greatest passion university students have during this stage of their lives is music. Listening to music is the thing they do most, besides studying. That's important to know—consumer psychology states that when we understand what motivates people and what their passions are, we can better connect with them.

HSBC wanted to change the perception of their bank (and banks in general) as stuffy, unhip, old institutions. To that end, they developed the *Zero Regret* campaign and created a hashtag, #zeroregret, to support it. They enlisted British rapper Lady Leshurr as their spokesperson, and she wrote a song, "Zero Regrets," with lyrics about things such as building confidence and not regretting the hard work that you do. They made a music video, which they launched on social media, and then created a separate "behind the scenes" video showcasing how students had been involved in the production of the original Lady Leshurr video.

The campaign was a huge success, in part because it resonated with HSBC's brand purpose, as expressed on their website:

Our purpose—opening up a world of opportunity—explains why we exist. We're here to use our unique expertise, capabilities, breadth and perspective to open up new kinds of opportunity for our customers. We're bringing together the people, ideas, and capital that nurture progress and growth, helping to create a better world—for our customers, our people, our investors, our communities, and the planet we all share.[3]

HSBC did everything right. They connected everything they did to their purpose. They collected insights and used them to build their brand and connect with their new target segment, millennials. They chose the right type of collaborator—someone with whom students could relate—to create a more authentic connection with their audience, and the campaign helped to grow a year-by-year brand consideration, which ultimately led to new customers.

This success is actually a mark of consistency: HSBC has developed quite a knack for connecting with young, tech-savvy millennials. In 2018, they launched a robot named Pepper at their Fifth Avenue branch in New York City. Pepper greeted visitors, answered their questions, and provided information about new promotions. And because Pepper was extremely photogenic, "she" generated a lot of media attention. The robot story went viral, and the feedback HSBC got was 99 percent positive. Pepper surpassed ten thousand interactions in less than ninety days—now *that's* engagement! The robot even increased interest in employment with the bank.

Better still, HSBC was able to collect data on how people would react to robots in their bank locations; that is, they were also testing and collecting data for the future.

The bank put Pepper to work because the executives realized that although they have strong brand recognition globally, they're not as well known in the United States. They also believed that robots (and technology in general) are the future of the banking industry, so they wanted to test a robot to see if it would drive engagement for their brand and help them stand out from all the other banks on Fifth Avenue. Retailers are always trying to give you a pleasant, innovative experience when you go to their brick-and-mortar outlets; think of the Apple and Nike stores and the exceptional experiences you have not just with their sales teams but with everything—the lighting, the aesthetics of the layout, how the products are displayed, and so on. HSBC wants to create an experience like that when you come to the bank.

Of course, HSBC isn't the first organization to realize that they need to target millennials or that social media is one of the best methods for doing so. Nor are they the only company to take an organic approach to reaching this valuable demographic. When FedEx was trying to figure out how to differentiate themselves from UPS and the United States Postal Service and how to capture millennials' brand loyalty, they conducted research to better connect with their target and found that millennials feel more connected to companies that do sustainability work.

Before building a campaign, FedEx tested different kinds

of messaging: FedEx is the fastest, offers real-time tracking, has the best rates, promotes sustainability throughout the world by reducing emissions and devising less wasteful packaging.[4] Of these various messaging strategies, the one that most resonated with millennials was the message about making the world a better place with their sustainability work.

Armed with this information, FedEx created a multi-channel campaign to emphasize how the company leverages its global network to make the world a better place. Before its launch, however, this multichannel campaign was subjected to substantial A/B testing, which is critical in marketing. Always test your message and make sure it resonates before you spread it across all your channels.

The delivery company then conducted extensive research to determine the most relevant digital channels to connect with their millennial targets. They found that Tumblr was the site where millennials spend most of their social media time and would likely be their biggest source of engagement.

The result of all this research and careful message testing was a phenomenally successful campaign—brand consideration went from 30 percent all the way up to 45 percent.

Over two decades, FedEx has created a successful overnight delivery model with high efficiency in their processes. All their capabilities—innovative, easy-to-use packaging; best-in-class service; centralized computer systems; tracking services that send real-time tracking information right to your phone— have been strengthened over time by the customer insights they are continually collecting. These insights tell them not only how they can best serve their customers today but also how they can better serve their customers tomorrow.

* * *

A FEW FINAL RECOMMENDATIONS ABOUT INSIGHT

In your data-collection efforts, don't neglect to utilize *all* the resources available to you. I often see companies failing to capture insights from their partners, suppliers, and other stakeholders. Remove the silos; collaborate with different teams (and even your customers!) when you are obtaining and collecting data.

Also, I can't say this enough: Test, test, *test!* Test your insights to make sure they're real and are going to be relevant. Then, once you've begun to act on those insights, continue to test your messaging and customer activities until you start seeing results. One of the most frustrating things I've seen in my consulting work is that we often have a lot of great insights to work from, but not much testing is being done. When an insight is not tested, the insight is not used correctly—and then projects fail.

Finally, never stop making observations. *There is no substitute for this type of data.* Sharp, meaningful observations are the first step toward deeper, more meaningful connections with your customers.

Every CEO wants to increase efficiency and productivity. Every CEO wants to strengthen engagement. But too many CEOs focus too intently on short-term return on investment.

It is not just how we obtain the insights for today's initiatives or today's projects that produces high ROI—it is how we take these insights a step farther to adapt to the future. Always be asking, "How do we collect additional insights today that will illuminate the future of the company—the future of our brand?" Companies that can align their messages with their core purpose will come across as more authentic and will have better connections with their customers.

KEY TAKEAWAYS

- Without insight, you're always vulnerable to unexpected external events.

- Combine big data and an anthropology approach to address gaps to capture consumers conducting tasks in context.

- Collect data and align it with your purpose to develop an effective marketing strategy.

- Test, test, *test!*

8

CHOOSING THE RIGHT COLLABORATION PARTNERS

It is literally true that you can succeed best and quickest by helping others to succeed.

—NAPOLEON HILL

COLLABORATION (both internal and external) is one of the most important, *necessary* strategies a company can pursue—and in my experience as a consultant, it's one of the most overlooked.

Many CEOs bristle at the idea that they need to form

collaborative relationships, especially with other organizations. To them, it seems like a matter of pride: if my company cannot do something on its own, and I have to partner with someone else to get it done, doesn't that indicate a shortcoming in my company?

No, not at all. In fact, it is common practice. If your goal is for your company to grow, become more flexible, and bring something new to your customers that benefits them and adds value to their lives, then it is only sensible to occasionally pool resources with other organizations if doing so will help to make that happen. Companies that team up either with their competitors or a company they do business with can bring new perspective to their organization and identify new opportunities. The partnership can reduce lead times, find gaps, increase brand awareness, and gain new knowledge.

Collaboration consists of bringing together people with expertise in different disciplines in order to generate new ideas and to lower production costs or the end cost to the consumer. Collaboration can help you reach new markets and can improve the overall efficiency of your operations and services.

Collaboration also makes it easier to find experts when you need them—people whose expertise you might need from time to time but not often enough to hire them full-time in your own organization—in order to create something new or improve your existing products and services. Collaboration can promote creativity, empowerment, and social interaction by bringing in different perspectives and by bringing organizations together.

EXTERNAL COLLABORATION

Later in this chapter I'll get into internal collaboration (something that too many companies neglect), but for now let's look at some examples of *external* collaboration.

Collaborating to Achieve Aims that Benefit an Entire Industry

In March 2021, IBM and Intel announced plans to collaborate on chip technology research in order to address a global shortage of semiconductors—a crisis that affects every industry from aerospace to automotive technology.

It's a good partnership match: IBM excels at semiconductor research and Intel is the world's largest semiconductor manufacturer.

According to analyst Patrick Moorhead, writing in *Forbes*,

IBM was responsible for the world's first 7nm chip with EUV and high mobility SiGE channel PFET. . . . Intel missed the ball on its 7nm and 10nm schedules . . . [a situation that the company] seems determined to rectify moving forward. . . .

These long-time competitors are now teaming up to advance process and logic technology, an effort many believe to be a move to advance U.S. semiconductor interests by combatting Taiwan-based TSMC. . . .

As IBM's Mukesh Khare put it during a Q&A on the topic, "It's great for the semiconductor industry and it's great for leadership in the U.S. to make sure that we continue to be the leader in semiconductor innovation." It's not often you see two historically competitive titans of the industry come together like this, and I'm very much looking forward to seeing the fruits of the partnership somewhere down the line.[1]

IBM and Intel each have their weaknesses, as both companies are well aware, but more important, they have complementary strengths. And if collaboration, even between rivals, can leverage those strengths to overcome both parties' weaknesses, then everybody wins, and the entire industry benefits and moves forward.

IBM and Intel are still competitors, of course, but competitors aren't the only entities a company might consider collaborating with. For example, look at the partnerships developing between the pharmaceutical industry and academia—especially between Merck and Johns Hopkins University.

Back in 2013, Merck announced that it was "right-sizing" (i.e., *downsizing*) its internal R&D operations, a move necessitated by falling sales. Other pharma giants, including Pfizer and AstraZeneca, had recently done likewise.[2]

These drug companies were facing a dilemma: tough times called for slimming down and cost cutting, but R&D, perhaps the most expensive aspect of their operations, was also the most vital. With R&D hobbled, how would anyone come up with the next Celebrex or Lipitor?

Enter the Academic Drug Discovery Consortium (ADDC), an association of pharma companies and universities, including Vanderbilt, Johns Hopkins, and UCSF, among others.[3] The universities are motivated by royalty streams that flow from these collaborations, providing much-needed revenue that can fund other research. Companies such as Merck and Pfizer, on the other hand, benefit by being able to shed an expensive burden in their pursuit of greater efficiency.

For Merck, one fruit of this kind of collaborative effort was a revolutionary new cancer drug.

Johns Hopkins cancer researcher Bert Vogelstein was having difficulty garnering support for the work he and his colleagues were doing—research that would ultimately lead to the development of the highly effective Merck product now known as Keytruda. Merck researchers had been working along similar lines but the project was not seen as promising and had been given a low priority.

So Vogelstein contacted Merck and made a proposal: Johns Hopkins would conduct the necessary studies *and* pay for them; Merck needed only to provide the drug, which at that time had not yet been approved for any kind of use. The result: in 2017 the FDA approved Keytruda for the treatment of a wide variety of different cancers,[4] and today Merck is making money hand over fist from it. Keytruda is on its way to becoming the best-selling drug in the world and is projected to generate $22.5 billion in revenue by 2025.[5]

Collaborating to Create Brand Awareness

The Enchantment Resort, an upscale hotel in Arizona, has an

ingeniously conceived partnership with a local Volvo dealership. The Volvo dealer provides cars for the hotel to offer its premium-package guests for the duration of their stay—and everybody benefits from this arrangement. The guests benefit by having the use of their own car—a brand-new Volvo—for any errands they may need to run, to visit Sedona's Red Rock Scenic Byway, or to explore the region's various national parks. No need to call a taxi or an Uber—this is your car for as long as you're here!

The hotel benefits by being able to offer this free perk—something their guests will remember the next time they (or people they know) are visiting Arizona. And Volvo benefits from increased brand awareness: the hotel's guests have the opportunity to test drive a Volvo for a week or two—and maybe seriously think about buying one.

Co-creation

The last form of external collaboration I want to talk about is co-creation, which is rapidly becoming a popular method for engaging with customers to generate new ideas, solve problems, and facilitate crowdsourcing.

The major benefit of co-creation is that it is customer-centric and allows you to adapt quickly to the market: the customer is participating in the creation or improvement of products or services. This adds tremendous value as it brings in diverse groups of people, fosters creativity, and promotes awareness ahead of a new product launch.

The way co-creation works is simple: companies look for consumers who are passionate about their brand, and they will sometimes even go as far as to look for consumers who have certain necessary skill sets to co-create with them. By doing this, companies are getting the customer's perspective and building a community for their brand. There is no better way to drive word of mouth than by building a community while you're creating something new.

Since the early 2010s, DHL has been holding workshops with their customers in Germany and Singapore, inviting them to help the company find creative solutions to problems and improve customers' experience with DHL. These workshops, which are called "Innovation Centers," enable customers to brainstorm with DHL employees and executives. One such workshop led the company to develop a drone called the "Parcelopter," which makes deliveries easier to accomplish in hard-to-reach areas situated in forbidding terrain. The program has been so effective (the company reports an 80 percent increase in customer satisfaction) that in 2018 DHL expanded it and opened a new Innovation Center in Chicago.[6]

INTERNAL COLLABORATION

External collaboration is *always* a great idea, but it's not the only way to collaborate—and not necessarily the most important. A business must never neglect the health of its capacity for *internal* collaboration.

When you have teams that don't work well together or

are unwilling to share their knowledge and expertise, you are going to have friction and aren't going to get the results you're looking for on any project connected to those teams.

Let's revisit an assignment with a pharmaceutical company that was a client of my firm. I mentioned we were working on a project whose purpose was to draw consumers' attention to the importance of preventive healthcare and healthy behaviors when taking over-the-counter drugs.

One of the things we needed to do to execute this goal was improve the company's internal collaboration. When you have a lot of portfolios (i.e., when you have a lot of brands within your company), internal collaboration is often overlooked or is not even attempted because leaders don't think they can get their teams to work together.

The first thing we did was to identify key stakeholders in their respective departments. We wanted to look closely at each unit within these departments and see which ones were best suited to collaboration on this project—and which departments' efforts would be wasted. The idea was to avoid including those departments that would not be adding any value.

As I have observed collaboration efforts among departments in various corporations over the course of my career, I've noticed that many of them just invite everyone from every department, without even looking at the time and resources these departments are going to spend executing a given project or idea. Three to six months later, they find out that the inclusion of certain departments led to wasted effort—they didn't utilize those departments' resources or those departments' input wasn't relevant to achieving the company's goals. The takeaway is that when you are conducting internal collaboration work, it is important to identify those stakeholders who are really going to add value.

It is also important to mitigate any tensions that may have arisen among the teams beforehand. High-performance teams tend to consist of highly educated individuals, especially in the pharma sectors—and such people are less likely to learn from one another and less likely to share knowledge.

Sometimes different teams have the mindset that they can stand out by outperforming other teams—or worse, that individuals on those teams can advance their careers by outshining their teammates—and that is where a silo mentality sets in. This should go without saying, but I want to emphasize it: make sure that your departments don't have a silo mentality when you are collaborating. It is important to clear any bottleneck so that everyone is aligned toward the same goals.

The most important thing is to have strong top-level executive support for the collaboration process. Executives need to roll up their sleeves and demonstrate their involvement, thereby setting an example. When an executive team member such as a VP comes in and says, "This is great! *This* is how we collaborate," their involvement is a constant reminder that everyone has the support system they need to properly execute their roles. Executive involvement also builds better relationships across departments and among teams.

WHEN SHOULD YOU COLLABORATE? WHAT ARE THE RISKS?

You should consider collaboration whenever you see that your existing offers are generating less growth than they ought to or when your organization feels it has the time and the resources to take risks and explore new ideas. You should consider collaboration when you find yourself asking, "What else can we do to provide value to our customers in new and exciting ways?" You should think about collaboration when your company already has three to five differentiating capabilities and you are looking for new ways to achieve a competitive edge.

Another sign that you should collaborate is when you see your competitors taking bold actions. If your competitors are pursuing acquisitions or they've come up with an innovative new product or are in some other way doing something new, then you should definitely start looking into collaboration with external partners. Leverage your existing capabilities—the strong ones—and use them to create a competitive advantage by partnering with a company that shares your values and might share your objectives within the scope of the proposed collaboration.

That's an important distinction to make when evaluating potential collaboration partners: *values*. I'm sometimes asked whether there are risks inherent to external collaboration, and my answer is that the risks lie in not looking closely enough at your prospective external partner.

When you are looking at external partners, you want to

determine whether your company and your would-be partner have similar values that you can focus on. Can you and the external company come up with something new that would benefit both of you in a way that will increase brand awareness and/or profits for both of you?

It comes down to aligning your mission and your values with that company and seeing whether you have enough in common to start that conversation. If you are completely misaligned on your values and mission, then you are not going to be able to collaborate well.

Customer insight is very important too. You don't want to go into a partnership without insight into whether the customer will even benefit from it. You want to make sure that your partnerships will create value, that you have some insight as to whether the customer will actually buy your products if you create something new with that company.

Above all, there needs to be a certain level of *trust* between the two companies—which brings us back to the matter of compatible values.

A lot of companies do not have that mindset, especially older companies. There was a time when most companies didn't want to collaborate because they were worried about rivals stealing their data or poaching their best employees. Trust was an issue. They didn't even collaborate internally because there was always competitiveness within their own departments: "We want our department to do better than the other departments!" Indeed, you can still see that attitude in siloed departments today, as I noted previously.

When it came to shared knowledge and shared resources, that mentality was the norm years ago, but today things are different. Today many companies are willing to be open and will share their research; when you are being collaborative, you have to be transparent. Of course, you obviously want to take whatever steps are necessary to secure your intellectual property and trade secrets, but you have to be able to share resources and talent and knowledge in order to collaborate. Ultimately, it comes down to a mindset that some leaders have and some don't.

Security

Collaboration with your suppliers and customers is much easier than collaboration with your competitors because sharing sensitive information will be a concern.

Today data security is top of mind in all companies. When collaborating, you should determine what level of risk is acceptable in your organization. Examine your data—where it's held and how it moves across your environment. Understand which risky activities are outweighed by their value and which ones are not acceptable. I once worked in a corporate organization where all zip file creations were tracked and extra permissions were needed to move or transfer the files.

It's important to make security a part of your business decision-making process. COVID-19 has pushed many companies to understand data security and get rid of their outdated tools. The pandemic has increased the data risk inherent in collaboration since everyone has been forced to work from home.

IP Protection

According to PricewaterhouseCoopers, collaborative innovation and intellectual property best practices include establishing ownership of knowledge and establishing how both parties will share risk and R&D expenses. Typically after a project is selected and during negotiations, teams from both companies will discuss the conditions of collaboration and governance concerning contracts and sharing intellectual property. After these discussions take place, research, pilot production, and commercialization phases can be conducted.

* * *

In working with large, midsize, and small companies, I've noticed that the large companies collaborate a lot more. The reason is simply a matter of resources. Large companies go to a lot of conferences and attend a lot of global events, and the things they see at those events spark ideas—such-and-such company is doing this, the other competitor is doing that, and so on. Larger companies are more likely to collaborate because they are more likely to have some type of national or global presence, which gives them access to more partnerships—they have already built brand credibility.

But collaboration isn't just a strategy for the big boys or for companies that have a lot of revenue and resources. According to University of California professor Andrew Hargadon, "Insights comes from outside." It's in the leader's best interest to "help their people connect to outside input."[7]

The preceding co-creation and collaboration examples are great ways for companies to select new projects, experience new learnings, and create bold new visions. Using start-ups is a great way to adapt to new markets and create flexible strategies that will help you reach a broader audience and connect to your purpose.

Midsize and smaller companies sometimes forget that they can do this. If you own or work for one of those companies, I hope this chapter has opened your eyes.

KEY TAKEAWAYS

- Collaboration can help you reach new markets and improve the overall efficiency of your operations and services.

- Collaboration makes it easier to find experts when you need them.

- Ideas come from outside and are pieced together to combine knowledge in new, innovative ways.

- Effective *internal* collaboration is essential for a functional organization.

9

CO-CREATING WITH YOUR CUSTOMERS

If I had asked people what they wanted, they would have said faster horses.

—Henry Ford

HENRY FORD NEVER SAID THAT.

That alleged quotation is often used to support the notion that the best path to success in business—maybe the only path—is to be some kind of singular, visionary prophet. The trouble is, it's entirely fabricated.[1]

In fact, Ford once actually said more or less the opposite: "If there is any one secret of success, it lies in the ability to get the other person's point of view and see things from that person's angle as well as from your own."

Alas, Ford wasn't very good at taking his own advice; he had a low opinion of the common man, and his company was terrible at listening to its customers. General Motors, in contrast, began to take a different attitude toward innovation in the 1920s, introducing concepts such as installment selling, used car trade-ins, and annual model changes. This enabled them to sell cars to market segments that Ford had ignored, and by the end of the decade they had eaten, well, not *all* of Ford's lunch but at least half of his sandwich. In 1921, the Ford Motor Company accounted for two-thirds of all US car sales; by 1927, they were down to a mere 15 percent.[2]

Nevertheless, Ford's attitude persists today in a lot of companies, to the detriment of their success. Yes, Steve Jobs did indeed say, "A lot of times, people don't know what they want until you show it to them." But few of us are Steve Jobs. For every world-dominating Apple in the marketplace, there are thousands of failed companies you've never heard of whose founders went broke trying to follow in Jobs's footsteps.

There's a better approach to product development than, "They'll want it when they see it," and that approach is *co-creation*, a concept I touched on in the previous chapter that we'll explore further in this one.

Co-creation, in a nutshell, means engaging with your customers to find out what they really want and then enlisting their help designing it. In chapter 7 we talked about obtaining insights by engaging with your customers, but co-creation is more than that.

Engaging with customers in order to gain insight is about collecting data. But when you co-create, you are getting customers' input to actually build something new. Co-creation is about forming a working relationship with your customers. Companies that do this go beyond collecting insights and work with their customers and shareholders to co-create innovation. Usually this is accomplished via an engagement platform, where customers and the brand can share their ideas and access knowledge tools to enhance their creativity. This platform needs to be inclusive, creative, and transformative.

So how is value created through co-creation? By integrating the company's existing resources with the customer's problem-solving input. Co-creation will allow you to form partnerships and will help you improve customer engagement and loyalty.

In chapter 8, we briefly covered DHL's co-creation program. DHL is not the only major company that engages in this practice: Nike, GE, Unilever—all of these companies (and many others) have already embedded the co-creational framework in their company cultures.

HOW CO-CREATION CHANGED NIKE'S BUSINESS MODEL

Just to give you a little background, Nike was founded in 1964 by a track-and-field athlete named Phil Knight and his coach,

Bill Bowerman. The company initially focused on making shoes for serious athletes—tennis shoes, basketball shoes, shoes for track runners, and so on. They hired employees who were runners, tennis players, or basketball players on the assumption that these were the types of people best qualified to develop the right types of shoes for specific types of sport.

This helped them develop new products and grow their company. But eventually the company became an internal echo chamber—Nike was relying on its own employees to come up with new ideas, and by the mid-1980s they realized this wasn't working. Nike's new products weren't exciting enough, and they just weren't competitive—their sales were basically stagnant. This may be hard for younger readers to imagine in 2022, but in 1985, Nike just wasn't a "buzz" company that anybody was excited about.

So they took a hard look at their organization: What are we not doing? What *should* we be doing? And in the wake of this bout of introspection, their focus changed. Up to that point, Nike had existed solely (pardon the pun) to make shoes for top athletes; henceforth, they would broaden their reach to appeal to the general public as well. Nike decided to put the customer first—to find out what consumers want and then develop products from there. One of the best marketing decisions Nike made was to sign an endorsement deal with Michael Jordan in the 1980s. The Air Jordan line remains one of Nike's biggest campaigns decades after Jordan retired from playing basketball, with its own website section labeled "Jordan," selling sneakers, jackets, clothes, and gear for all ages and genders. This decision has led to so many impactful marketing strategies for their brand. The Jordan deal illustrates that Nike has always observed and listened to their customers.

To that end, they started collecting customer insight, and they embarked on a series of co-creation efforts. In 2006, they introduced Nike+, an activity-tracking device designed in collaboration with Apple that pairs with the customer's iPhone. The device is inserted into a shoe and it measures and records the distance and pace of a run and also estimates the calories burned. Online forums hosted on Nike's website enable users to share ideas, challenge one another, and provide Nike with useful feedback. At around the same time, the company introduced a platform called Joga.com (*joga* means "play" in Portuguese) to collect ideas from soccer fans, and they incorporated information and ideas gleaned from that platform into their soccer shoes.[3]

Nike has come a long way since its inception in 1964 as a niche company serving athletes. Today, thanks to these co-creation efforts, they have become the global leader in the footwear market—a feat they have accomplished by focusing on inclusivity in their product pipeline, offering different sizes in women's workout clothes and children's shoes, and by answering the public's demand for sustainability by using recycled materials to make sneakers.

Nike cofounder Phil Knight once said, "We used to think that everything started in the lab. Now we realize that everything spins off the consumer. And while technology is still important, the consumer has to lead innovation. We have to innovate for a specific reason, and that reason comes from the market. Otherwise, we'll end up making museum pieces."[4]

Knight and Nike understand that the external landscape is constantly changing and eventually the lab isn't enough; that is, eventually the lab won't produce what your customers want. The majority of Nike's sales come from regular consumers: moms and teenagers—not athletes. These customers don't care about the perfect shoe the tennis player needs. When Nike became aware of that gap, they understood why they weren't growing anymore, and they started talking to the customer. When you are customer-driven in how you make your product, you will achieve the long-term security of knowing how to give consumers what they really want.

THE PREREQUISITES FOR CO-CREATION

So what are the essential elements you have to have in place for co-creation to work? First, you need to reflect on your values—are the customer's needs your top priority? You also need organizational agility; an entrenched, inflexible company culture will serve you poorly. (Remember, *think like a street vendor!*)

What else do you need? Briefly, you need leadership engagement, a willingness to share information, a commitment to your marketing program, and, most important, a willingness to accept results that confound your expectations.

Leadership Engagement

For co-creation to succeed, leadership definitely has to be involved; if you're going to make important changes to the way your company operates or the nature of products or services you offer, then the people who make those decisions need to be on board and engaged.

It is important for leadership to be proactive and to understand key drivers of the market in order to make intelligent decisions. Top management may also need to be willing to incur some costs in the co-creation process, depending on the complexity of your project.

It's equally important to consider the experiences of all the stakeholders who will be involved in or affected by the new offering. When the customer says they have an idea, your production and sales teams—the folks who are going to make it and the folks who are going to market it—all need to have a say in deciding whether to pursue it.

Willingness to Share Information

Dialogue between the brand and the customer helps you with prototyping (i.e., you need to see if your customers actually like the new product), and that helps to minimize product failure. Organizations that are reluctant to share information—or even to engage in communication and dialogue with their customers— cannot process value co-creation; customer participation is one of the prerequisites of any value co-creation process.

Commitment to Marketing

Nike's success at co-creation is due in part to the tremendous job they do at marketing, and marketing and co-creation go hand in hand. The process works only if a critical mass of your customers is aware of the program and excited about it.

Nike also has a robust online presence, and that makes all the difference in the world. I've written in previous chapters about the importance of technology and social media, so I won't belabor that point here—but I do want to remind you of it.

Openness to Surprises

Co-creation will often yield results very different from what you *think* you are looking for, but getting answers from the customers' point of view—answers you may not have been expecting—is the whole point. Remember that you're beginning from a different starting point than you may be accustomed to. You are creating something brand new and are relying on your customers to create the ideas behind that new thing, and those ideas will differ from anything your internal development mechanisms have previously produced.

Again, the entire point of this exercise is to think of things you didn't think of before.

MY OWN EXPERIENCE WITH CO-CREATION

To illustrate the importance of some of these points, I want to describe an assignment I had with a lip balm company a few years back.

This company, a unisex lipcare brand, was competing with multinational companies in the beauty market, but it was a much smaller company just trying to gain some market share. To that end, it decided to pursue a co-creation strategy and it enlisted me to make it happen.

Its intention, initially, was to get its customers' input to determine what new flavors they'd like to see because the market trends we'd seen indicated consumers wanted a choice of flavors. Rather than rely on the best guesses of our marketing people regarding the flavors that would sell well, we thought, *Why not just ask the customers what they want?*

This was the company's first co-creation effort. One of the biggest challenges most brands face is being attractive enough to be noticed amid all the noise within its industry, and the company thought a co-creation project would be a great way to connect with its customers. The project was budget friendly, so if it didn't work out, it wouldn't be the end of the world. (The social media platforms we were using were not costly, and the project wasn't terribly time-consuming.)

We started by utilizing social media channels to learn where our customers hang out and where they have conversations about beauty—specifically lip balm. We engaged these communities and posted an invitation to join our conversations to participate in our co-creation process to pick a new flavor for us.

Once we'd identified our customers, we asked them to share

their experiences. We wanted to know more than just their flavor preferences, so we posted specific questions such as, "What do you want your lip balm to feel like? What do you want it to smell like?" After that, we let them take over the conversations—and the ideas they contributed went well beyond flavors.

We received thousands of responses, which we shared with our product development team in real time in order to get their feedback. Our customer community told us what they wanted, not only in terms of flavors but also how they would like the product to feel on their lips. Other responses focused on packaging, which surprised us; respondents said the plastic wrapped around a tube of lip balm shouldn't be so hard to open.

After we collected and analyzed all the data, the product development team came up with four new flavors, a variety of textures, and easy-to-open packaging.

The result of all this co-creation process was a deeper, more trusting relationship with our customers. This helped us increase awareness of the brand, which in turn improved distribution and boosted sales. When you co-create with your customers, you empower them by enabling them to express exactly what they want *and* to help create it. Now you are building a closer relationship between the brand and its most engaged customers.

One reason this worked so well for us was that we had *engagement* at every level of the organization, from leadership on down. We involved the marketing team—in fact, the idea *came from* that team. The product development team was involved—we asked for their input on all customer-generated ideas. More importantly, the C-suite was involved, and they gave us the authority and flexibility to use whatever resources we needed.

Best of all, the project was budget friendly—we did not spend any money on fancy platform tools or even to build a platform ourselves to do this. We just used regular social media channels.

Finally, we were open to surprises. If not for our customers' unexpected input, the company would have gone no further than adding a few new flavors.

THINGS TO CONSIDER BEFORE DIVING INTO CO-CREATION

Some questions to think about: What motivates the customer? What will motivate them to be involved in this process? The customer will decide what is valuable when they submit their ideas, and that's where the value comes from. Management needs to continuously monitor these engagement activities on their platform and to intervene with customers if they're offering irrelevant information or blatantly impractical ideas.

Keep industry trends in mind. Are the trends slow and predictable or are they changing quickly? Also keep your own goals top of mind. Do you require only a small innovation boost or do you need to shake up the industry with something completely new? In the case of the lip balm company, we were just looking for a small innovation to stay competitive. The company knew it needed to do this because it had noticed an industry trend: other companies were offering different flavors and colors with their lip balm products. You want to know what your competition is doing. You should also be prepared to take risks and be open to new ideas that reframe how you serve your customers.

Nothing is ever guaranteed, so don't neglect testing. At bigger companies, when you get to the prototype stage (or close to it), projects sometimes fail because focus groups look at the prototype and say, "Nope, this isn't what we wanted." This gives you an opportunity to quickly tweak the product before you invest a lot of time in marketing it. We gave free samples of our lip balm rather than just going straight to launch; we didn't know if anyone would be excited about any of those flavors or if they would even sell at all. Testing is important in co-creation. Nike does a lot of pilot testing in markets such as China before bringing new innovations to the US market.

The customers who will be your co-creators also need to be knowledgeable about your product. You don't want consumers participating if they don't understand how the product is used; otherwise, the information you glean from the process will not be valuable.

I recommended that you *not* offer your customers any monetary rewards or prizes during a co-creation process. You are looking for authentic participation. You are looking for true fans who love your product already and want to enhance it. You want consumers who are naturally motivated by intrinsic rewards because these folks will be better engaged and will therefore add more value.

The final barrier to overcome is your own preconception of what it means to have a "customer" to collaborate with. Many of you may be B2B (business to business) operations—but co-creation isn't just for B2C (business to consumer) companies; many B2B companies do co-creation work. Ultimately, *any* end user should be considered a customer, even—in fact, *especially*—if that customer is also a business. For example, Netflix has numerous B2B co-creation strategies that support its B2C offerings. The streaming giant has often formed partnerships with studios, directors, and actors—and perhaps most presciently (and profitably!) it has invested in technology start-ups such as Roku.[5]

* * *

We know that customers seek inspiration. They want to be entertained, they want to be challenged, and they want to be involved. If you engage with your customers, they can give you ideas that might otherwise never have come to you and can even assist in product development. You put the customer at the center of your process, you listen to them and observe them, and then you work from there.

Co-creation efforts will make your product innovation more adaptable and increase your speed to market by leveraging direct engagement with consumers. You don't need lots of expensive resources and tools to do this. It can be very easy. Ultimately it's simple: just ask your customers what they want. They'll be happy to tell you!

KEY TAKEAWAYS

- Co-creation efforts will make your product innovation more adaptable and increase your speed to market by leveraging direct engagement with consumers.

- For co-creation to succeed, corporate leadership has to be involved.

- Co-creation will often yield results very different from what you *think* you are looking for.

- When you are customer-focused, your company will be able to maintain its long-term success by giving consumers what they really want.

10

RIDING THE S-CURVE

Developing New Expertise and New Ideas

Here is an uncomfortable truth: In time, everything in your life, as you know it, will perish . . . especially . . . your business.

—MAGNUS PENKER[1]

THERE YOU HAVE IT. Sorry to be the bearer of bad news, but as you can see from this quotation, Magnus Penker thinks you're going to die.

163

As Neil Young sang, "Rust never sleeps." Yesterday's innovation is now today's business as usual—and tomorrow's obsolete dinosaur.

These cycles are predictable. An *invention*, if it is accepted and catches on in the market, becomes an *innovation*. This growth in popularity visualized on a graph creates the upward direction of what's known as the S-curve. Eventually, however, that popularity peaks—often because someone else has invented something better—and the curve crests and falls.[2]

This curve is inevitable; it's not even necessary for someone else to build a better mousetrap (although eventually, someone usually does). In the end, growth will plateau simply because competition has entered the market after noticing the success of your initial innovation.

In the *Inc.* magazine piece from which the chapter opener quotation is taken, Penker emphasizes the importance of developing new ideas and new expertise. The upward portion of any S-curve will not continue indefinitely, and if you're not primed to jump to a new curve—if you're not always focused on continual innovation—you will become obsolete. And then you'll die.

THE THREE HORIZONS

Penker and other experts—myself included—recommend that companies employ McKinsey's Three Horizons framework. This model, first introduced in the 1999 book *The Alchemy of Growth*,[3] provides a structure that encourages businesses to pursue potential future growth opportunities without neglecting or compromising their performance in the here and now.[4]

The idea is that when looking to the future, business leaders must keep their eyes focused simultaneously on three separate horizons, and innovative businesses must always be starting at least one new S-curve on each of these horizons.

- Horizon One ideas are short-term, concerned with improving and fine-tuning the existing business model and its existing products and services.

- Horizon Two ideas concentrate on ways to take that model and those products into new markets.

- Horizon Three is about developing entirely new capabilities to create or respond to new opportunities or to be ready for anticipated disruptions in the future.

In fact, McKinsey's own reflections on the Three Horizons model, from a 2009 online article, echo the theme of *this* book—being prepared for the unpredictability of the future. "The framework continues to be useful, especially in uncertain times. The immediacy of concerns around horizon-one businesses can easily overwhelm other efforts important to the future of a company."[5]

It's about building ideas for the future, not just for today. We can see examples of Three Horizons thinking in some of the stories in the previous chapters of this book; the co-creation projects undertaken by companies such as DHL are really about conceiving and collecting ideas for Horizon Two and Horizon Three.

Or consider Pepper, HSBC's Fifth Avenue robot from chapter 7. While Pepper was talking to customers, she was also subtly testing the public's response to the idea of interacting with robots. HSBC was collecting information to use for future projects that might help them better connect with their customers.

And don't forget Porsche's SUV. That was certainly a Horizon Three initiative; they didn't know whether their customers would even want such a vehicle.

Amazon is a stellar example of Horizon Three thinking. How do you take an online bookstore and expand it into a different market, let alone capture segments of completely unrelated markets? Yet Amazon bought Whole Foods—a mostly brick-and-mortar operation—and successfully turned it into an online grocery store as well.

I have often coached clients into thinking about Horizons Two and Three. In chapter 2, I described my work with a financial firm that wanted to attract millennial clients—that's the very definition of the kind of future-oriented thinking that characterizes Horizon Two!

FUJI FINDS A NEW S-CURVE

As I hope I've made clear, you want to avoid a "growth gap"—a situation in which a company fails to understand that its current product/services will one day cease to be relevant, and therefore the company will not grow or expand. (Pharmaceutical companies stand firm here. They understand this as a matter of course because they know the patents on their drugs have an expiration date, after which the generic drug companies will copy their innovations.)

Whatever disruptive ideas you come up with, it's important that they not be geared toward short-term ROI. To maintain the endless series of S-curves that Penker recommends, you need *sustainable* ideas for the long-term future. Growth, rather than short-term profit, should be the focus.

Let's look at Fujifilm as an example. Around the close of the twentieth century the company saw a huge decline in sales of their cameras and film. In his book *Innovating Out of Crisis*, Fuji CEO Shigetaka Komori candidly discusses the photographic film industry's failure to cope with how quickly digital cameras became a trend.[6] Although Fuji had anticipated the coming market shift toward digital cameras as far back as the 1980s, the collapse of the photographic film market, when it came, happened much faster than anyone had expected. Komori quickly realized his S-curve was diminishing—so he devised a plan to save the company from becoming obsolete.

They reviewed their capabilities, conducted an inventory of their technology, and saw opportunities to adapt to new markets including the pharmaceutical industry, the cosmetic industry, and electronics (e.g., LCD screens). In the field of cosmetics, they were able to leverage their experience with gelatin, an ingredient in photo film production derived from collagen. Fuji also had deep knowledge about the oxidation process that causes photos to fade over time, and they were able to apply this expertise to remedy the effects of aging human skin.

Komori emphasizes the importance of the action that is required once the new goals are communicated. In his book he references the words of a famous Japanese admiral: "Do it and show it; say it and tell it; have them try it; then praise them, and they will do it by themselves."[7]

In other words, show your employees how the job is done. Many companies don't provide the support or coaching employees need to move forward. It's important for the organization to align around a common point of view in order to respond effectively. Employees need to know that they'll be supported when they are conducting experiments. The role of a leader is to simplify complexity and provide clarity about key priorities and the "why" of what you are doing.

Today Fuji makes a wide variety of consumer products, from digital cameras and binoculars to skincare products (and, yes, film), but they also have a range of business products, including medical systems, graphic systems, motion picture products, recording media, industrial semiconductors, and more.

Kodak, on the other hand, failed to take these kinds of actions quickly enough. A Kodak employee actually developed the technology to allow cell phones to take pictures. Kodak management wasn't interested; whoever heard of taking pictures on phones? You took pictures on cameras, not phones! Oops. Kodak declared bankruptcy in 2012. What made the difference for Fuji? It was Komori's decision to find ways to apply the company's existing technologies and strong capabilities in other arenas. How do you take such specialized knowledge and expertise and put that capability to use someplace else? It takes a thorough inventory of what you know how to do and a comprehensive understanding of other markets. Perhaps more important, though, it takes a visionary willingness to look so far into the future that you're *prepared* when a disruptive new technology comes along to threaten your business model.

A DIVERSE CULTURE

So how do companies develop new expertise and new ideas? One way is to foster a diverse culture of different people with different knowledge and expertise. We talked about culture quite a bit in chapter 6, but I want to briefly return to the subject here. In the following example, I describe the importance of diversity used by NASA, which ultimately enables teams to look at new ideas at the intersection of disciplines or when people with different perspectives look at the same problem to reveal new opportunities.

In October 2020, John Saiz, former chief technology officer of NASA, appeared on Magnus Penker's monthly Innovation 360 webinar. It's important, Mr. Saiz said, "to ensure that you have inclusive leadership in place. . . . leadership that actively solicits ideas, seeks diverse perspectives, and supports experimentation. That fosters a work environment where all the employees . . . feel valued; they feel welcome; they feel integrated. Communication [and] inclusive leadership—those are probably the two most important things."[8]

Saiz went on to say that over the years, as NASA expanded their culture to include a more diverse assortment of people—not just demographic diversity but also different types of expertise—they had more successful missions and conceived more innovative projects. NASA made culture a priority, and they frequently benchmarked and took organization-wide surveys to look for opportunities to be more innovative. One of their key cultural assessments showed that inclusion was vital to innovation, so they quickly made this a priority to add to their core values. As Saiz points out, inclusion builds trust, openness, and accountability, so a company that is open-minded and inclusive will be more collaborative.

It starts with leadership and setting an example. Successful organizations understand that in order to innovate, you need alignment between your leadership style and the impact you make on your culture plus an openness to including all employees. That's a vital element. When someone at the executive level gets involved in a new project or a new idea or any kind of transformation, corporate culture responds to that commitment.

THE CORVETTE "SKUNK WORKS"

One of the most important requirements for a healthy culture is *trust*. You have to trust your people to do their jobs well and make good decisions without micromanagement—you have to give them autonomy and independence and let them do what they need to do. This imperative is best illustrated by the story of Harley Earl, the automotive designer and executive who gave the world the Corvette.

Earl noticed that World War II veterans coming back

from Europe had developed a taste for the hot little sports cars that were widely available over there (MGs, Jaguars, Alfa Romeos, and so forth) dominating postwar European road-racing circuits. Yet GM was utterly opposed to making anything along those lines. It bothered Earl that American consumers had no options other than big, boxy four-door sedans.

But a few rogue executives wanted to compete with the European sports car makers, and in the early 1950s they created what they called "the Skunk Works," a secret, padlocked design lab. GM execs were kept in the dark about this operation until the time came to reveal it. Earl and his accomplices literally had to steal parts and fake invoices from other GM divisions so that he could get this car designed, completely behind the backs of his bosses.

Think about that for a moment: Corvette became one of the most iconic cars this country ever produced, a car whose aesthetics defined postwar America, yet it was done completely behind locked doors. It would have been so easy for Harley Earl *not* to do this—and therein lies a lesson about culture. GM's culture lacked flexibility, and the company failed to place sufficient trust in its best people; because of that, we almost didn't have the Corvette!

I can promise you that if Symmetri Consulting had been around in 1953, Earl would never have needed to resort to a secret "Skunk Works." Culture mapping could have told GM that its culture was too stiff and rigid. If you're not flexible, you can't create new things.

We use a culture mapping tool to plot key factors that

apply to most challenges faced by most organizations. This cultural map helps you decode how your culture influences day-to-day collaboration and how your people respond to change. We identify the kind of culture you have, and from there we determine what your possibilities are: what can you do with the culture you have? If you want to change that culture, we show you what you can do and how you can do it.

A NEW INNOVATION PROCESS

How does a company explore new ideas and new expertise? Many great ideas can come from consumer insight—consumer segmentation, needs, trends, and brand equity. This data can be further dissected to map out the "who, what, why, where, when" of the topics. Companies can also tap into qualitative research, social media data, cultural insights, consulting experts, and even semiotics.

We encourage our clients to think about McKinsey's Three Horizons via our ideation workshops. Before placing your ideas in the right bucket, look at the technical and executional uncertainty versus the market and organizational uncertainty. Furthermore, an ideation process needs to be followed by incubation, in which the idea is prototyped, tested, shown to customers, retested, validated, and moved forward. It's rare that the first version of an idea is the one that actually makes it to the market.

Companies really struggle with the incubation part of the process. The incubation process allows for learnings that include experience, opportunities to hear different points of views through discussions, and documentation of the knowledge learned to create future actions. The experience can be transformative for teams involved in this process. Like a street vendor, teams can learn and practice entrepreneurial methods that favor prototyping, testing, and rapid iteration. This is why incubation periods are important—they are necessary for finding product and market fit.

Ideation workshops can lead to true creative breakthroughs if they're done right. To ensure a wide range of perspectives, companies should curate a group that is as diverse as possible in terms of work experience. It's important for companies to create a safe space for radical ideas. When participants vote on new ideas, they often choose the ones that seem most feasible and workable, but it's important to allow participants to vote on radical and practical ideas separately. With the help of AI, there's no need for brainstorming sessions that take up so much time and energy. Instead you can use ideation tools, which will cluster your ideas into categories and transform the original idea into a more viable option. Hypotheses are important to the process of refining ideas. They allow you to test your hypothesis quickly and efficiently in smaller experiments, which can give valuable feedback for future searches on a larger scale. A successful workshop should have a concrete action plan to follow up on the ideas put forth. This could include which team will be assigned ownership of that specific project and what data is needed before moving forward with any plans as well as identifying constraints if there are any limits or strengths within your industry in regard to this particular idea.

Successful companies never let good ideas (such as Harley Earl's Corvette!) get thrown away. At Microsoft, for example, they give their employees a safe environment in which to ideate and share their ideas.

* * *

When you're developing an innovation process, look at external factors: What does the competitive landscape look like? When you have a new idea, scenario planning and culture mapping allow you to see if you have the resources to support it. Do you have the right in-house expertise and is your culture aligned in the way it needs to be?

After looking at your capabilities and the market, start filtering it down: Do you have the budget for it? If you don't have the budget for it today, can you create a budget for it for tomorrow?

Can ideas fail? Of course they can. But when ideas fail, you *learn* from them. The goal is to fail the right way when you're experimenting—to learn from that failure and use it to improve your ideas or reframe the hypothesis you're writing. According to Jeff Bezos, "Failure and invention are inseparable twins."

INNOVATION ADVICE FOR SMALLER COMPANIES

Large companies have a lot of resources, time, and money to explore ideas. For smaller companies, however, innovation can be more challenging, so I'd like to take a moment to explore those challenges.

Make no mistake—if you're a small company, you *can* do these things; you just need to do them in a smaller frame. Obviously you can't explore a hundred ideas because you don't have the resources to support that much ideation and research. So you do what you can with what you have. If you want to pursue an idea, what capabilities do you need to make stronger? What talents are you missing? Maybe you just need to hire two or three key people to fill in that gap. Often half the battle is just identifying the gap between what you have and what you need. The important thing is to make sure the company is always growing. When you successfully launch a new idea or a project, you want to make sure you are already building the next S-curve.

It comes down to practice and incremental improvement: a marathon runner spends months training their body to handle the physical stresses involved—you don't wake up the morning after a McDonald's binge and expect to finish a marathon. The goal is to slowly build up your body, exercising properly and eating the right nutrients under the supervision of the right coach. You have to have the right mindset and the right focus, and you need to have discipline.

It's the same with innovation. You have to have the discipline to practice and improve in order to find the disruptive ideas you're looking for. Once you've had that practice, you know what you've been doing wrong, and you can make improvements to your culture.

* * *

Since we cannot make perfect predictions about the future, companies have to learn how to innovate; just getting by is no longer an option—and will lead to extinction.

Maybe you don't believe me. Maybe you're balking at the thought of all the hard work involved rethinking your innovation process. Why should you work so hard always to be just at the start of yet another S-curve? What's the payoff for learning to be continuously innovative?

The payoff is that your company won't die.

Change happens quickly and the future is unpredictable. If you don't develop new expertise and ideas, you will die, as did Kodak and Circuit City and Blockbuster—companies that saw the new trends arising and didn't react quickly enough. Sadly, even when you *do* react, it is sometimes too late because by the time you figure out how to compete, someone else is already doing what you ought to have done. And then it becomes hard for you to survive.

I can't say this enough: it is urgent today for companies to simultaneously think not just about ideas for today but also about ideas for tomorrow. Do this because you want to stay relevant. Do this because you want to stay competitive.

Because one of those ideas will become a new growth engine.

KEY TAKEAWAYS

- An invention, if it is accepted and catches on in the market, becomes an innovation.

- Look for a new S-curve every two to three years by building the next set of distinctive capabilities.

- Fostering a diverse company culture leads to a diversity of new ideas.

- If you're not flexible, you can't create new things.

PART III
Making the Most of Your Technology Spend

11

OVERCOMING YOUR FEARS ABOUT BUSINESS TECHNOLOGY

A little fear is okay; it helps you determine which risks are worth taking.

—**Anonymous**

IT'S 2022, NOT 1982. This far into the twenty-first century, you'd think every business in the world would understand the importance of technology to its ability to compete successfully—or even to survive.

Yet a surprising number of companies still fail to understand this and are not looking into technology-driven strategies. Why? What are they afraid of?

The problem isn't confined to a single sector—these blind spots appear across the board, in nearly every industry, although some are lagging further behind than others. Technology-oriented industries, obviously, tend not to have this problem. The industries that are *really* behind are transportation, government (especially the US Postal Service), health care, and manufacturing. Many manufacturing companies are using out-of-date software.

If yours is one of those companies that takes an apathetic, indifferent attitude to technology trends, then you're speeding toward a cliff with a blindfold on. And after the couple of years we've just had—a global pandemic, riots, and political instability on a global scale—that devil-may-care mindset is a luxury you can't afford. We don't know what next year's challenges will bring, but we can't expect to be prepared for them if we're behind the times on technology.

Just to be clear, I'm not suggesting that a technology-driven strategy is useful only—or even primarily—as a hedge against life's vicissitudes. It's also a necessity today, in the here and now. Technology helps companies differentiate themselves in the market very quickly. For example, Walmart used technology to differentiate themselves in the retail market space in the 1980s. They were one of the first companies to use a barcode scanner; the idea, initially, was to increase efficiency throughout their stores. But this innovation eventually led to other technological advances, and Walmart's processes soon revolutionized supply chain management itself. How were they able to do this? By adapting their innate capabilities to the latest technological trends.

Bravo for Walmart—but they're not the only well-known company to achieve that kind of revolutionary change. Netflix did something similar. At the turn of the century, as streaming tech became more viable, they took advantage of their existing capabilities to leverage this new technology in a way that would forever alter the way the public watches both movies and television.

FOLLOWING THE TRENDS

What did Netflix do? First, they looked at their capabilities: They had a highly profitable subscription membership model. (Remember our discussion of this in chapter 3?) They had savvy IT integration, and when the new technology for streaming services arrived, they built it into their existing business. Putting their customers first, they offered a customized, user-friendly experience.

Finally, they completed their customer engagement by enabling curation and personalization—as a customer, you can create your own Netflix experience, deciding the kinds of content you want to watch and how and when you want to watch.

The upshot of this investment in technology is a fantastic customer experience, all because Netflix took the time to invest in a technology-driven strategy—and because they paid attention to technology trends. It was this attention that gave them insight into what was possible and the kinds of opportunities those possibilities presented.

I want to ask business leaders today: Are you following the technology trends? If not, *why* aren't you following them? Following technology trends can spark ideas and ideation processes, which can lead to the discovery of yet-unexplored opportunities.

What are those trends? Some of today's biggest technology trends include facial recognition, mobile content delivery systems that detect fraud, robotics that can be used to automate jobs (especially in the manufacturing sector), edge computing to process time-sensitive information, and quantum computing to help you dig through huge amounts of data.

Quantum computing is attracting companies to explore, build algorithms, and ramp up investments to *prepare change*. Although the full benefits of quantum computing are not here yet, companies are using R&D to see how they can embed it into their internal processes or improve their product development processes. An example of a company using this technology is Cloud Pharmaceuticals, a North Carolina–based pharmaceutical company. Cloud uses a Quantum Molecular Design process to combine AI- and cloud-based quantum computing to create new drugs. Traditional drug discovery methods are too expensive and have a high rate of failure. Some of the work done using this technology is to pick compounds that bind with biological targets and have good "drug like properties."[1] The process is more efficient than traditional methods due to the fact it doesn't require screening of already existing molecules. Cloud's compounds are ready for preclinical development, come at a lower cost, and enjoy a faster time to market.

The company has won first place in the US-China Health Innovation Competition. COO Don Van Dyke says that Cloud "continues to show leadership worldwide to enable pharmaceutical companies to cut 5-6 years from the process of early design of novel therapies."[2] The company is also collaborating with GSK to help design molecule agents to GSK-specified targets.

In a nutshell, a technology-driven strategy that aligns with your core capabilities can help your business offer a better experience for the customer, go to market faster, and compete with much larger enterprises.

* * *

Some believe that this slowness to adapt is a product of fear and that some CEOs' fear of technology is a function of their age or background. Many CEOs come up from finance, accounting, manufacturing, or some discipline other than technology, so they don't know much about it. So is there a culture gap or an age gap that creates a sense of distrust or discomfort around technology?

I don't think so. In my opinion, it is not a culture or age gap at all. It is not just younger CEOs who take technology seriously —a lot of older CEOs are interested in it as well. Also, while many CEOs come from finance, sales, or project management, there are nevertheless quite a few who have tech backgrounds.

So it's not age or culture. Rather, I think the issue is an awareness gap. Some people simply are better at staying on top of trends, and this talent is not confined to any one age cohort. The CEO who is looking into technology is always customer obsessed and thinking about market trends. If you're that CEO, you are aware of how the customer's tastes, preferences, and expectations change and evolve. You are aware of the new technology that came out just last week and why it is making an impact and why people are talking about it. Those are the CEOS who are thinking, *Is this something I should look into? Should we incorporate that new technology? Is that a service we should be providing? Which industries are using it, and* how *are they using it?*

Failure to ask those questions is dangerous. I've talked to folks from different industries who have worked in big companies, and some of them have candidly said, "You know, we missed the mark. We were asleep at the wheel." These are large corporations I'm talking about—not just small or midsize companies. These organizations have the capabilities, the resources, and the money, yet they missed the boat. They are not number one in their industries; someone else is. And why is that? Because someone else is more aware than they are.

When you fail to ask the questions you need to ask and when you think of a new tech product as a fad that will go away, that's when a competitor swoops in and takes advantage to become the leader in that market—*your* market. That's what happened to Kodak and Blockbuster; both companies saw things happening right in front of them but didn't take action.

Many companies don't understand the difference between a fad and a trend. A fad is behavior that is adopted by a population for a short time; it's misleading and claims universal acceptance. The fad drops once the perception of novelty is gone. Companies can utilize short-term fads in tactical marketing efforts to create awareness of a product or program, demonstrate the timeliness of their organizations, and attract new audiences. Examples of fads include Beanie Babies, fidget spinners, Angry Birds, Pokemon Go, iPod Nano, Napster, and Google Glass.

A trend, on the other hand, is a real, long-term change that is driven by customer needs and solves a problem. Trends require the company to create organizational strategy. Examples are the increase in the use of social networks, quitting smoking, and usage of mobile phones.

BlackBerry is a perfect example of this. There are stories that BlackBerry insiders looked at the iPhone and said, "It's a cosmetic thing. It's pretty, but business leaders are not going to use iPhones."

I think we all know what happened after that. When your internal conversations are like that, you are missing out on what really is going on outside your window. You don't collect data, you don't see that the new thing is gaining momentum, and you take no action—and then, all of a sudden, you're gone. Like BlackBerry. (Yes, I know the company isn't really *gone*, but its signature product has ended up in history's trash bin, and the company itself is a lot less valuable than it was in 2002.)

NOTHING TO FEAR BUT FEAR ITSELF

In the interviews I have conducted during my assignments, I've found that most company executives are scared of innovation, and the reason is that they are ROI-focused. They don't pursue long-term projects because they don't see the value in something that is going to take three to five years to develop with no certainty of ROI.

It comes down to fear of failure—they don't have the necessary confidence to innovate. It's not just fear of technology but a fear of trying to do something new. For example, if you are looking at AI machine learning and you want to incorporate that into your technology-driven strategy, how are you going to get started? You don't know anything about machine learning. You need to be able to understand how it is going to benefit your customers and how it is going to differentiate you from the industry.

When a new technology appears, there are going to be leaders who say, "That's not for us." But they don't even really know what it *is*. That's why it's vital to be knowledgeable, to understand what that new thing is and how it can be utilized in your industry.

That said, obviously there is research involved; you can't just jump on any shiny new thing and implement it and expect it to work. You want to see if it fits in with what you do, if it fits into your core values and delivers value to your customers or your partners or creates efficiencies in your operations.

When I was working with the pharma industry, one of

my roles was to serve as a scriptwriter in the IT department, helping implement a new inventory database. I was in the manufacturing division and larger companies with manufacturing divisions often don't have the most updated technologies (even though those companies are billion-dollar companies!). This is especially true in the health-care space—another industry that is in danger of being left behind.

After the system was completed and launched for training, we got a lot of negative employee feedback about user experiences. They complained that they couldn't find data easily, that there were too many search layers, and that they had log-in problems—when you went to different sections of the database, you needed to have a certain type of access permission.

When I asked the manager why didn't we just install a brand-new software platform that integrated everything rather than build this database on top of another database, she told me, "We don't know how to use the newer systems that are out on the market. They are too complicated. It takes too much time to test and integrate them. Plus, if the project doesn't show a quick ROI, the senior management team will not approve the new technology." So they went with a cheaper version of a database and just piled onto the existing databases that we already had.

What we were doing was adding more complexity to our system by adding new databases on top of older database systems—a highly inefficient way to work. This made user access slower and made it hard to remain updated with new inventory. Worse, the new system was likely to fail because it didn't integrate well with the older systems.

Another common objection I hear is, "Our culture is too rigid to adapt to new technology." This is not an excuse at all. Yes, some cultures are not as flexible as they should be, but you can take baby steps to get where you need to go. Start with internal updates—updating your internal software with the newest technologies so you can streamline your processes. Your employees will quickly see the benefits of this, and that experience will make them more amenable and willing to adapt to further technological changes.

When the Innovation 360 Group, a consulting firm based in Stockholm, surveyed five thousand companies on their use of technology, they found that companies using technology-driven strategies are more likely to achieve sustainable and profitable long-term growth. Adding a technology capability can help you devise new business models, form new partnerships, and create better connections to your customers. Technology can enable cost-efficient operations and provide diverse revenue streams, just to name a few of its benefits.

FIRST CONSIDERATIONS

I discuss two types of technologies in this and subsequent chapters: industrial technology and informational technology. *Industrial technology* is embedding technology to combine engineering and manufacturing to make production faster, simpler, and more efficient. *Information technology* is using physical devices such as computers, storage, networking infrastructure, and processes to create, process, store, and exchange all forms of electronic data.

In other words, industrial technology is to improve internal processes and enable people processes. Informational technology is customer-facing technology to enable better customer experiences.

When thinking about technology-driven strategies, whether to better your services to the end customer or even to implement internally, you should start with the question, *What is the end result going to accomplish?* For example, if you are trying to implement a cloud-based service, you want to ask, "How will a cloud-based service deliver value to the customer?" What pain points is the new technology going to resolve?

For an internal implementation of technology, you ask pretty much the same questions. "How does it deliver value to my employees and to my entire operation? Does it reduce cost? Does it produce efficiency?" Trying to implement a new technology simply because your competitors are doing it is not a good starting point. Yes, industry trends are important, and market trends are important to understand and follow, but you want to look at the trends, and you want to see how the new tech applies to the core DNA of your organization.

Then you want to ask, "Do we even have the necessary talent to be able to support this new technology?" It's important to align your goals with your current capabilities when thinking about new initiatives.

And of course, the most important question concerning internal readiness is, *Do you have buy-in from senior leadership?* (More on that necessity in a bit.)

* * *

One final note about "first considerations": once you've decided to adopt a new technology, you'll need to select a vendor to provide it. When you are considering partnering with a technology firm, you need to look at transparency, data security, governance, and other risk-related concerns. The last thing you want is to open your company up to data hacking or ransomware attacks. Fortunately, many reputable Internet security companies can help you eliminate or minimize such risks, and a little research—not just googling but also consultation with your peers—will lead you to a company that is a good fit.

"WE CAN'T AFFORD IT!"

Is technology expensive? That's too vague a question. Too expensive for what or for whom? It depends on the size of your company, your resources, and what your goals are. If your company has deep pockets, then obviously you can do something bigger. But smaller or midsize companies have to look at their budgets and see what's possible.

Regardless of your size, however, you can do a lot on a smaller budget just by shopping around; many companies offer cloud-based services, IoT sensors, and so on, and you can always go to a smaller firm to get what you need at a budget-friendly price.

Technology is not the crazy spend that it might have been twenty or thirty years ago, and this is partly because important advances of the last few decades have proliferated. Most industries today are already using cloud-based technology. Many manufacturing industries are starting to use IoT services. IoT in one form or another has been around for over thirty years. When it first appeared, only very savvy companies were interested in it, and only very large companies with a lot of money could afford to pursue it. But today IoT is accessible to nearly everyone. The takeaway from this is that technology that has been out for many years tends to be affordable.

More important, however, *a carefully considered technology purchase will be a profit center and not simply a cost.* A technology that benefits your customers will make you more competitive. And an internal technology update that benefits the organization will be a cost savings because it will make your operations efficient.

This is where buy-in from senior leadership becomes a big deal. Brett Bonner, the now-retired vice president of research and development for the Ohio-based supermarket chain Kroger, says it's important, when considering investing in any new technology, to secure the CEO as your sponsor—but it's even more important to have the CFO as your collaborator.

Bonner knows what he's talking about. Kroger today is using edge computing and IoT technology, which for them takes the form of devices in their supermarkets to provide real-time shelf information. The purpose of these IoT devices is to ensure food safety by monitoring temperature control in the produce department so that less product has to be thrown away. They are also monitoring traffic in their stores. Kroger serves 9.5 million shoppers a day, so imagine how much data they are collecting with this technology.

You have to be well informed when investing in technology. You want to make sure to spend your technology budget wisely. You want to ensure that it is going to deliver value for the customer as well as your organization. Therefore, you need to ask yourself how you are going to use it. How is it going to deliver that value? And you want to be mindful of the cost because technology can add up quickly.

* * *

Everybody agrees that the customer is of the utmost importance, but in my opinion, customer care and technology go hand in hand. So if the customers and what you want to deliver for them are important to you, then you need to reach them where they actually are. You need to meet them on their own terms, and the way the customer consumes information today is through technology. It doesn't matter what business you are in—manufacturing, health care, transportation, or whatever. Everyone who interacts with your business—not just your customers but also your suppliers, partners, employees, UPS guy, everyone who is working with you—consumes information through technology, and they want you to make communication easy for them.

Consumers use technology to do their grocery shopping. They use the Internet to search for the things they need. So if you don't have a good inventory system and a good database that integrates with that system, then everything becomes a little harder for your partners, your employees, and all of your other stakeholders.

The lesson I want you to take away from this chapter is this: *Be open to technology.* Don't fear it. First conduct research on your customers and understand fully how it is going to help them and how it is going to change your industry. Before investing in the newest trend, ask yourself, *Do our customers even have a need for it or will it help to optimize our internal processes?*

Then write your goals. If you want to use this tech, what outcome would you want to see from it? How would it deliver value?

Is it going to deliver value to the customer?

In the case of the medical device company assignment that I described in chapter 3, we already had data indicating that the subscription model was going to work and our clear intention was to put IoT sensors on the components that go to the hospitals. When you have all the data you need, the next question becomes, *How are we going to implement it?*

When we first met with the medical device company, it wasn't sure how to use the data; it didn't know if its plan was going to work. We took the company through one of our workshops and determined that there was interest. *It looks like the customer can benefit,* we thought, *and there is going to be value in it.* But how are we going to implement it? What are some of the challenges that we're going to face? Are the sensors going to work? Are they going to attach correctly? And while we were doing all the legwork of collecting enough data to make sure that the simpler pieces of the plan were going to work, we were also collecting data on what kind of pricing we could get for this new subscription model: Are the customers going to go for it? Are the hospitals likely to change?

So you start off with basic questions like these and then you start brainstorming. You start looking at how you're going to understand what the market is and how your components are going to fit into it. Is that idea even worth pursuing? Is that something that you can collect data on—enough data to come back and say, "This is something that we can do"?

Once you've made that determination, what would the business model look like? What flexible options do we have by using this technology? Do we have an audience? Is there a market? Is this going to work? *How* is it going to work? Do we have the resources we need? Brainstorming isn't easy, but it's necessary to ask yourself how you plan to deliver your product or service successfully. The key isn't the technology itself; rather, it's the delivery and creativity—which ultimately lead to a great end result for your customers.

Hopefully this chapter has given you some basics to think about in terms of making technology a central aspect of your business strategy. Of course, in order to do that effectively, you'll need access to strong technology expertise—and as we'll see in our next chapter, you'll want to keep those experts close at hand.

KEY TAKEAWAYS

- If you take an indifferent attitude toward technology trends, you're speeding toward a cliff with a blindfold on.

- Following technology trends can spark ideas and ideation processes, which can lead to the discovery of unexplored opportunities.

- When you assume that any new tech product is a fad that will go away, that's when a competitor swoops in and takes advantage.

12

HIRE A CTO

Why You Must Solve
Your Technology Challenges In-House

It's a CEO's job to manage boards, not the other way around.

—BILL CAMPBELL[1]

WHEN YOU HAVE technology problems, whom do you call? Do you immediately reach out to the IT team at the external marketing agency you use?

Stop doing that.

Think about what you might be able to accomplish internally using only the in-house resources already located within the walls of your office. External factors such as the COVID-19 pandemic can always disrupt your marketing efforts, but if you have an in-house digital team, you can sustain those efforts with little or no agency cost.

The pandemic has pushed many companies to reevaluate where and how they spend their marketing dollars, and many have ended up cutting their agency partners loose during this time. Your company can still launch new services and craft communications to engage with your customers—but only if you have an in-house team. You can use technology to do more work with less budget. Things such as machine learning and data-driven insights create greater efficiencies in your marketing strategy and improve the speed at which you operate and react to unexpected events.

THE TWIN IMPERATIVES OF A CTO AND A TECHNOLOGY STRATEGY

For the last three decades, technology has been reshaping every industry and transforming how we do business. As I said in chapter 11, this means that a technology-driven strategy is no longer optional. It's *essential* that you have a tech expert on board in the C-suite. If you don't already have one, you *need* a CTO—a chief technology officer.

Over the course of my career, I've seen dramatic changes in the background requirements for the C-suite: while once the only serious prerequisite was financial literacy, today it is *digital* literacy that is most imperative. An effective CTO can identify new areas where value can be created, lead a new culture that supports a technology-driven strategy, and align the organization's business strategies with its technology strategies.

When I was working in corporate, I saw the challenges faced by companies that didn't have internal technology experts. In one instance, I was working on a project for a pharma company, and we had gathered consumer behavior data relating to a specific brand. But when the time came to determine how to best utilize this data, it soon became apparent that our internal team did not have sufficient digital literacy to properly leverage it. They didn't know how to ask the right questions about the data or how to make informed decisions that would align with the company's overall strategy. Instead, the director relied on agency services to provide recommendations.

And a year later, our marketing efforts using that data had produced no ROI.

For any strategy to be successful, your business decisions need to be aligned with the data you are looking at, and you need experts who can understand that data. Just as important, those decisions also need to be aligned with the company's brand, its goals, and its values, and this kind of alignment is very difficult to achieve with an external agency.

Don't get me wrong: there's a lot to be said for outside agencies. Agencies already have the in-house talent to understand and interpret the data in ways that your own C-suite executives can't do if they don't have a background in technology. And when you're working on smaller marketing efforts, small campaigns, and things such as that, you can definitely use external agencies. You also don't need an internal digital technology expert to address day-to-day activities such as newsletters, website updates, and a basic social media presence; that work can be done by a smaller external team.

I'm also not saying that you should shoulder the expense of full in-house media and creative teams or that you should have under your own roof every kind of team you can think of that a creative agency has—you don't necessarily need those.

But you do need to have some technology expertise in the building, and you need people who have data science backgrounds. If you don't have anyone within your organization with the talent at least to understand the data you gather in the course of your customer research and scenario-planning activities, then that data is useless.

Companies that are using technology expressly to differentiate themselves should definitely have technology experts in-house. Too often, I've seen the following in companies where I have worked: you have data but no one in the company knows how to translate it into actionable terms, and you are forced to rely on the agency's advice on how to use that data to move forward. This is not a good thing.

When you have someone at the C-suite level who understands the data you're collecting *and who also understands the company's mission, purpose, and strategy*, then—and only then—can you make informed decisions. Agencies can help you with strategic planning and creativity, but strategic planning requires alignment with your company's overall strategy. Your own executives will know what your company's strongest capabilities are and how to leverage them. An agency will not have the in-depth knowledge that enables you to best utilize your unique capabilities.

Perhaps the most important thing a CTO can do is formulate a *technology strategy*—that is, a tech strategy that is separate from your overall business strategy and focused entirely on how technology will be used by your organization to further its larger objectives. A technology strategy will define the role your CTO plays in your organization; it will clarify what business objectives can (or cannot) be achieved by the use of technology and how various devices, applications, and services should be used. The CTO can think of it as creating a technology portfolio in three categories: deciding whether to put R&D into a product, direct customer-facing processes, or updating internal processes.

Formulating a technology strategy is, of course, the responsibility of your CTO, but that person *must* have the support of the CEO and the board of directors. It needs to come from the top: the CEO needs to communicate the strategy to everyone so that there is buy-in at all levels of the organization and everyone's work is aligned with your technology strategy, which in turn must be aligned with the company's overall strategy, its goals, and its mission.

You need to see this as primarily a leadership issue—both the manner in which you promulgate your technology strategy *and* the decision to adopt that strategy in the first place.

If there is no company-wide technology strategy, and a brand or division within the company wants to try to adopt a technology strategy on its own, it is going to have a hard time aligning it with the company's larger business strategy. Even if you have a manager who has some background in technology, that person's expertise goes only so far in terms of translating it to value. What do you do with data? How do you align business decisions with the company's goals so that you can create value?

The bottom line is this: if you want your technology strategy to have market value, then it needs to be understood and have buy-in at all levels of the organization, from the top all the way down.

SUCCESS STORIES: GM AND DOMINO'S

Let's look at a couple of companies that took strong, proactive steps to make sure they could handle all their tech issues without relying on external vendors.

In 2018, GM decided to stop outsourcing their IT department, having realized that in order to be 100 percent focused on their business, their technology employees needed to be in-house. Since then, they've seen their IT department produce 10 percent more business value and innovation than would have been generated by outsourcing IT to an external company.

One step they took in the course of their transformation was to implement a private cloud. That decision was an expensive one, but it saved them numerous future costs and dramatically reduced redundancy and complexity.

You need a lot of resources to set up something like a private cloud. Most companies use a public cloud-based service. That means you hire a company such as Microsoft that provides cloud-based services, and that outside entity helps you manage the work and—hopefully—create efficiencies. The important difference using a private cloud is that only your company's direct employees have access to it: you have full control of your own cloud service—which is a tremendous asset in terms of security, among other concerns. (Of course, once you've implemented such a system, obviously you need to hire team members who understand how the cloud works—a subject we'll get to shortly.)

In order to make this in-house IT transformation happen, GM implemented it on a self-funding basis, reducing its use of contractors to pay for hiring new employees, consolidating twenty-three data centers into just two, streamlining applications and tools for portfolios, and automating tasks to reduce costs. By downsizing to free up money for their IT transformation, GM was able to identify numerous areas where they could save money—all by implementing a strategy that would itself save more money in the long run.

* * *

A great technology strategy starts with an involved board of directors. For a stellar example of this dictum in action, look no further than Domino's Pizza, whose stock price has risen from $3.85 per share in 2008 to $478 as of July 7, 2021.

So what did Domino's start doing differently that accounts for this impressive rise? They hired technology experts to redesign the way they deliver pizzas. They created apps with text messaging capabilities linked to mobile phones and smart TVs, and they used customer data to redesign their business strategy.

In interviews with CNBC's Jim Cramer and other financial journalists, former Domino's CEO Patrick Doyle described the enterprise as, essentially, a tech company that sells pizza. That may be a tad hyperbolic, but it's not far off the mark: the company has conceived a number of technological innovations, such as the "pizza tracker" that tracks a customer's delivery in real time, and they have used technology to enhance the customer experience by improving ease of ordering.

Doyle moved on to pursue other opportunities in 2018, but Domino's is still looking to the future. For several years, the company has been "investing aggressively" in driverless cars, which may one day prove faster and more reliable than human drivers.[2]

Besides making the company's service more attractive to the public, all this tech activity helps Domino's collect more customer data since the company does not outsource their delivery as Pizza Hut and Papa John's do. As a result, because they were early to market with these innovative online services using technology, Domino's now controls 50 percent of the online pizza market.

Where did the idea for this brilliant technology-driven strategy come from? I can't claim to know that with certainty, but according to their website, Domino's counts as a member of its board of directors a man named C. Andrew Ballard.[3] Ballard is the founder of an investment firm that focuses on software and technology and is also the vice chairman of Zignal Labs, an

SAS-based media intelligence software company that manages communication and measures consumer opinion in real time.

Make of that what you will, but if Ballard has exerted the kind of influence I suspect he has, then this is a perfect demonstration of how the presence of internal experts at the C-suite and board level can change the direction of a company for the better.

In chapter 9, I quoted Innovation 360 CEO Magnus Penker on the necessity of always developing new ideas and cultivating new expertise—and *this* is what Penker was talking about. Sometimes it is not enough to make incremental improvements and produce small innovations. Sometimes you need to do something truly radical to stay competitive.

And that's what Domino's did. If they hadn't undergone such a huge transformation over the last decade, their stock price today wouldn't be $478 a share.

WHAT TO LOOK FOR WHEN YOU'RE SEARCHING FOR TECH EXPERTISE

So why don't more companies install technology experts in positions of authority at the C-suite level? Is it because too many CEOs are older and aren't technology-minded? That depends on the size of the company. At larger organizations, I would say that's not the case. Executives in these companies tend to be pretty savvy, and they understand the importance of technology-driven strategy—it's what keeps them competitive. But at some of the midsize or smaller companies, if the CEOs there are much older, then yes, failure to adapt to changing times is often the problem.

Today many companies are preferentially hiring millennials, who are extremely digitally savvy—online is how they like to do business, whether that business is finding new vendors or creating new relationships.

Obviously, "hiring millennials" doesn't count as a fully developed technology-driven strategy, but it's a start. A younger, more tech-savvy staff can at least provide some kind of baseline-level internal support system and give you confidence that at least some of your employees have already adapted to whatever new digital technologies are presenting this year's challenge. Millennials came of age during the turn-of-the-century technology revolution. They're comfortable with tech, know how to use it, and feel strongly about making sure that every business has an e-commerce presence, not just a brick-and-mortar retail store.

That said, I'm not terribly optimistic about the future of any company of any size that doesn't have a full-time, in-house CTO. If you're a smaller company, that pessimism may induce some anxiety. You may worry about the cost of this kind of digital transformation—any CTO worth his salt can command quite a hefty salary, which translates into a big commitment on your part.

With respect to cost, a lot depends on the size of the company. Most of the companies I work with are large companies, but if I were to recommend an in-house IT team to a smaller firm, the recommendation would be based on the resources that company has at its disposal, and on how much value is expected to be created by the new position.

It's not just a matter of resources; it is also a matter of talent. You need technology *experts*—people with data science backgrounds, people with technology and software engineering backgrounds. If you don't have a fully realized in-house *team* but still have access to other in-house talent with that kind of background, that is still valuable because those are the people who know how to start conversations about how to move forward, how to best utilize your website data, and other issues of that nature.

* * *

Having technology or digital experts in-house helps you fill the technology gap in capability development. It helps you become a coherent company with a diverse set of talents and leadership styles, which plays a vital role in building the company's capability systems. It creates a source of value that enhances internal efficiency, effectiveness, and alignment. It will easily help you reinforce other strategies by merging the skills and perspectives of businesses and technology leaders to drive new transformations. It will also allow you to conduct more experiments, transform outdated platforms, and launch new customer-facing flexible capabilities.

Equally important, having a technology strategy will reinforce your capabilities, make you more adaptable, and competitively differentiate you in the market—which brings us to the subject of the next chapter: using technology to stay ahead of your competitors.

KEY TAKEAWAYS

- If you don't already have one, you definitely *need* a CTO.

- Decisions need to be aligned with a company's brand, its goals, and its values—and this kind of alignment is very difficult to achieve with an external technology agency.

- If you don't have anyone within your organization who can understand the data you gather, then that data is useless.

13

USING TECHNOLOGY TO STAY AHEAD OF YOUR COMPETITORS

AI allows us to put one step in front of a hypothesis, a driven sign, so we're flipping the model. Instead of the hypothesis creating the data, in the Berg approach we allow the data to create the hypothesis.

—Dr. Niven R. Narain[1]

THE LAST THREE chapters suggested that we pay more attention to advances in technology—and you can be sure that your competitors are doing just that.

Mobile, analytics, social media, cloud computing, and other technologies have fundamentally changed today's business landscape. Companies are investing heavily in technology and learning how to lead with transformation enabled by that technology. Technology can help companies differentiate themselves from their competitors, and it can enable impactful engagement with customers. It can save costs, enhance operations, and increase efficiency.

And all of that adds up to countless opportunities to run circles around your competition.

HOW TECHNOLOGY CAN DRIVE TRANSFORMATION

In chapter 3, I described an assignment I once had to develop a data-driven subscription model for a medical device company; the company used IoT sensors to its its hospital customers' usage of its medical components, which enabled the company to better serve those customers by more accurately predicting their needs.

This innovative use of technology contributed to a dramatic transformation in the way the company did business—a transformation I was proud to be a part of.

In the next couple of pages, I'll show you some other examples of companies that were able to effect transformative changes, either by developing new technology, adopting existing technology, or devising new ways to put technology to use.

Intel

Perhaps the most transformative field of technology today is AI. Intel has created a neuromorphic research chip called Loihi, which enables a computer to learn and distinguish among various odors with far greater accuracy and sensitivity than a human being can manage, even "in the presence of significant noise and occlusion"—that is, other, stronger odors that would prevent a human nose from distinguishing less powerful scents.[2] The underlying technology that makes this possible is called *neuromorphic computing*, and it works by using analog circuits to mimic the structure and behavior of neurons with the aim of making AI work less like traditional computers and more like the human brain.[3]

The practical applications for public safety, medicine, and other fields are potentially huge. Loihi can detect chemicals that signal the presence of weapons or explosives or of hazardous conditions in an industrial setting. It can also detect biological odors that may indicate to doctors in the future whether a patient is suffering from an otherwise difficult-to-diagnose medical condition. Loihi can detect the presence of narcotics more reliably than a police dog, and it may soon be used to make more reliable smoke, natural gas, and carbon monoxide detectors for homes.

After Intel built this chip, they launched an awareness campaign to create a buzz about their exciting new discovery. That campaign quickly bore fruit: media attention came quickly from magazines such as *MIT Technology Review*, which is read in C-suites throughout the corporate and tech worlds and has over three million unique monthly visitors. This attention was soon followed by articles in the *Wall Street Journal, Forbes, Fortune, CNET*, and other media outlets.

So what is the business purpose of this chip and Intel's campaign to create awareness of it?

Intel is already a billion-dollar company but that doesn't mean they can just sit back and rest on their laurels. The company is working with academia and a diverse assortment of industries and partners to collectively overcome the wide-ranging challenges facing the field of neuromorphic computing. They are looking for ways to stay relevant and competitive as a forward-looking leader in the AI space. Accordingly, they're looking for leaders who are interested in investing in AI.

The awareness campaign has generated tremendous opportunities for Intel to collaborate with other companies— companies that are seeking the kinds of Horizon Three ideas we talked about in earlier chapters of this book. Given the near-limitless possibilities of this new invention, any company that partners with Intel to use their new research chip will find themselves well positioned to solve a host of customer problems and create radical innovation in the market.

And all that work has paid off: after their awareness campaign, Intel saw a 77 percent increase in partnership inquiries and collaboration proposals related to neuromorphic computing.

Amazon

A few years back, Amazon launched Amazon Go, an innovative

new concept for a grocery or convenience store. Customers can enter the store using their phones to enter a locked turnstile that unlocks when you scan a QR code, "buy" their groceries, and then just walk out. A combination of technologies—including computer vision, deep learning algorithms, and sensor fusion—tracks shoppers' movements throughout the store, detects when merchandise is taken from the shelves, charges the customer's credit card, and sends a bill via the Amazon Go phone app.[4]

The first Amazon Go test stores were opened for Amazon employees in Seattle in 2016. Today there are twenty-nine Amazon Go locations open to the public in New York, Chicago, San Francisco, Seattle, and London—and with the customer-insight data they've collected in the last five years, they are taking this concept one step further.

In 2020, Amazon announced its intention to sell its automated "Just Walk Out" checkout technology to retailers. The company plans to mainstream the idea of shopping without checkout lines. According to a Reuters article from March 2020, one venture firm estimated that the market for retail without cashiers could grow to $50 billion, and Amazon's vice president of physical retail and technology stated that the size of the market would be determined by shoppers' preferences.[5]

Amazon's strategy shows they are using both information technology and industrial technology to enable better customer-facing processes. Their strategies define how well they have developed their internal capabilities, especially with regard to sensors, computer vision, and deep learning. When Amazon Go was launched in 2016, what were researchers doing? We've talked about this in previous chapters: they were—and are—collecting data. Every time you shop at an Amazon Go store, the company learns a little more about what you like to buy.

Obviously they were collecting data for years before they made key technology decisions, and their data gathering will continue to inform the decisions the company makes in the future. Should we plan on building five hundred Amazon Go stores? Or five thousand? Or should we be selling our technology to retailers so they can use it?

What makes sense for Amazon? What is the cost factor? What are all the things they need to think about on how they can best utilize this technology and take it one step further?

And that is all Horizon Three thinking—collecting, exploring, and exploiting data to ascertain what course of action best suits your company's strategy.

Nike

I recently ordered a pair of Nike sneakers for my son. They weren't just any sneakers; these were custom designed. We picked the color, the design, and the performance features he wanted before purchasing the sneakers on Nike's website.

So how is Nike using technology here? What they are basically doing is taking two different capabilities and bringing them together using digital technology; they are using their channel capability (i.e., the use of their website to make purchases) and their design capability (by offering custom design features). Nike didn't have these capabilities in place when they started their business in 1964; they developed them later, when they saw a way to utilize their capabilities in a new and different fashion.

This customization allowed a direct-to-customer (DTC) strategy, incorporating on-demand production and delivery capability to bring in more profits. This e-commerce platform allows Nike to reach customers in areas that do not have a Nike store nearby and to further expand its distribution channel to support their e-commerce presence.

United Overseas Bank

The United Overseas Bank is based in Singapore, but they have over five hundred branches in nineteen countries. When the bank decided they wanted to compete in the already crowded small-and-medium-sized-enterprise (SME) market, they knew they'd need to break through a lot of noise in order to get noticed.

Asking themselves, "How can we use web content to connect better with these smaller and medium-sized businesses?" United Overseas spent about twelve months collecting data on the SME-related content that appeared on the websites of its competitor banks. They used AI and machine learning technology to sift through all this data, sorting through content topics and formats to determine what messaging styles were preferred by SMEs. These tools allowed them to aggregate the data, benchmark their own content against their competitors' content, identify target audiences, and then identify opportunities to maximize the impact of their content.

The results were surprising: only 9 percent of SME engagement was with content actually created by banks. The other 91 percent of SME engagement was with content created by nonbanks that didn't even discuss banking at all. Instead, United Overseas' research showed that SMEs preferred content about market trends, networking, and employee development. They also found that these small businesses preferred written content to video—which was great because written content doesn't cost a lot of money to produce.

This data revealed a big opportunity for United Overseas Bank to better engage with SMEs *and* differentiate itself from their competitors—so they started to create content that would align with what these small businesses were looking for.

The result: they saw a 120 percent increase in traffic to their website, a 300 percent increase in marketing quality lead conversion, and a 770 percent growth in product page conversion.

In a nutshell, the bank used AI and machine learning technology to obtain insights into customer preferences, which suggested a competitive strategy they could use to engage with consumers and bring more business to their bank. United Overseas Bank is using technology to better enable their internal processes so they can be more intelligent and better prepared to go to market.

The story of United Overseas Bank, like the Nike, Intel, and Amazon examples, demonstrates that continuously innovating and using technology to build on momentum will drive growth for your company.

THE VALUE OF DATA

The example of United Overseas Bank offers an eye-opening lesson for any business that wants to get noticed in a competitive world: we tend to think that customer engagement happens because people are interested in what we have to offer—but that is often not the case. We often make assumptions about what consumers want, and then it turns out they want to talk about topics that are completely different from the ones in which we've been trying to engage them. But when you utilize the power of technology to collect data, you can quickly and efficiently discover what your customers *really* want.

This clearly shows you the importance of customer data— and from my experience working with dozens of companies, I can tell you that data is still not being utilized as it should be. Not every company is utilizing data to its best advantage, and that missed opportunity is why many companies are struggling to get ahead or even to compete at all. The Amazon Go example showcases how much a company such as Amazon values data. Amazon has been collecting data since the inception of their business, and they continue to do so today.

Obviously, Amazon has the resources to truly optimize that data, but you don't need to be a monstrous corporate behemoth like Amazon to benefit from technology and data collection. Bigger companies have an advantage because they have more resources to deploy, but smaller companies have advantages of their own because they are nimble. You have less complexity in your organization if your company doesn't employ five thousand people.

A smaller company can use technology to enable better strategies and can often implement technological strategies a bit faster because it has less data to sift through. Bigger companies have to sort enormous amounts of data and clear myriad operational hurdles, making sure all the different divisions are in line and that the company's culture is aligned with whatever the C-suite is about to propose to the market. Smaller companies have just that little bit of an advantage—less complexity—and may therefore be able to go a bit faster to market with new services or new products using new technology. If you're a smaller company that is not afraid of technology, that can help make you a little bit more competitive—or a lot more competitive.

WHAT YOU CAN (AND MUST) DO

If you've been slow or timid about embracing new technology, it's time for you to stop hiding—the future is coming whether you're on board or not. And if you don't embrace a technology-driven strategy to obtain and maintain an edge over your competition, it's only a matter of time before that competition outpaces you. As the saying goes, if you're not seated at the table, you're on the menu.

This needs to be a top-of-mind concern—always. Too many CEOs are held hostage by the kinds of fears we talked about in chapter 11, either because they don't understand how new technology will help them solve problems or because they don't have the necessary awareness of the different types of technology out there. They are worried about failure or that a technology upgrade is going to cost too much money and is not going to work. Many of them hesitate simply because they don't have the right in-house talent—but remember, you can always hire the talent you need.

Technology also makes collaborative efforts (the importance of which should be plain now that you've read chapter 8) much easier to pursue. I am a member of a community called Science Says, a UK-based platform that links members of academia with the business world. I've found it to be a great resource both for communities to collaborate, to learn, and possibly to co-create. You can talk to biomedical engineers or to people who are working on AI technology. You can talk to PhD students who are working on new research and have conversations to see whether what they are doing applies to your industry and how you can collaborate with them. The possibilities are limitless—I can't recommend Science Says highly enough.[6]

According to cofounder Beatrice Zatorska, there is a need for more applied research—less than 2 percent of current tech development comes from scientific research. Where is the remaining 98 percent? Too much research is going to waste while massive problems persist in health care, education, and climate change—problems that can be addressed only with the help of science. The problem is in communicating that research to nonexperts, and the whole process of collaboration between industry and the institution of academia is broken.

Separately, the general public demands reliable, fact-based information that can come only from scientific research. One indicator of this demand can be seen on Twitter: 47 percent of all

Twitter users follow scientists. People are fed up with fake news (fake science news in particular) and know scientists are people to be trusted.

* * *

After your customer data insights and your collaborative partnerships have made it possible to develop some new, disruptive, breakthrough technology, you'll need to get the word out to the public and drum up interest in your new products. Jeffrey Moore and Malcolm Gladwell, in their respective books *Crossing the Chasm* and *The Tipping Point*,[7] both recommend that you make use of what Gladwell calls "mavens"—early adopters who spread awareness by word of mouth (which, of course, nowadays mostly means social media).

"Mavens," "influencers," or whatever you call these folks tend to have certain characteristics in common: they like to challenge the status quo, enjoy looking for ways to influence society, care about community, and want deeper social connections. Many of these influencers use data science and digital media tools that can provide insights into consumer decision-making behaviors. This is important because when you are introducing new technology, as Amazon did, you want to find customers who are willing to *try* your new thing, and then you want to see what else they are willing to try. And when you're following your segments and seeing what else they're doing, it gives you a better idea of whether your new strategy is likely to work.

* * *

Technology can be used to drive efficiency and to improve operations, distribution, support, and process innovation. Technology-driven strategies can have an immediate impact, and that impact can sometimes be very large, depending on the nature of the innovation.

When contemplating a technology-driven strategy, first think about how it is going to create value for your customers and your company, and then use technology to enable it. The key is to leverage technology that aligns with your company's strategy in a unique way, not to copy technology solutions that are already being used in the market.

Technology is essentially an enabler for customer insights. The technology is the *how*; it is not the *what*. It is *how* to get that customer information, or *how* to connect better with the customer, or *how* to create better experiences for your customers.

That's all technology does; it is just an enabler to make life easier for everyone and to create more efficiency and flexibility for your company. If you are struggling to differentiate, or if you don't know enough about your customers, look into any type of technology strategy that promises to make transactions easier or that helps you understand more about what the customer is doing and why they are doing it.

In the next chapter, we'll discuss how you can leverage technology to make the world around you a better place.

KEY TAKEAWAYS

- You may not be paying attention to advances in technology—but your competitors are.

- The most transformative field of technology today is AI.

- Identify your business strategy first, design your customer experience from the outside in, and then invest in technology.

14

USING TECHNOLOGY TO DRIVE SUSTAINABILITY

Not a day passes for me without seeing the many ways in which digital technology can advance peace, human rights and sustainable development for all.

—ANTÓNIO GUTERRES

SECRETARY-GENERAL, UNITED NATIONS[1]

YOU'VE PROBABLY HEARD the term *sustainability* so often that it's lost all meaning. But when we talk about sustainability in a business context, does it mean anything at all? The short answer is yes. In this chapter, I'd like to explain why understanding and embracing this concept is vital to the health and future of your business.

Sustainability refers generally to the capacity for the earth's biosphere to support human life and civilization in the long run. Contemporary usage also has implications for human rights, in the context of what generally constitutes ethical, sustainable business practices. In short, *sustainability* is essentially a synonym for the more familiar concept of "corporate social responsibility."[2]

Once upon a time, companies had a responsibility to stockholders only to maximize profits and share price. No longer. In today's world, companies have a responsibility to take notice of climate change, massive carbon dioxide emissions, water quality, and overconsumption of nonrenewable natural resources—and the technology that has been developed to deal with these problems is allowing companies to innovate faster and become more efficient.

Regardless of whether *sustainability* means anything to you, you can be sure it is important to a significant portion of your customer base. Therefore, it is in a company's best interest to start pursuing sustainability efforts as quickly as it can. Sustainability needs to be treated as a business concern. Everything should be analyzed with this imperative in mind— your supply chain, your logistics, your operations, and even your sales—because the public and your customers are watching.

And if they don't like what they see, it is your business that will no longer be "sustainable."

THE DEMAND

Before we get into the benefits of sustainability-oriented tech, I want to address any objections you may have if you're not already on board with sustainability itself. I can hear what you're thinking: *"As an executive, I understand the importance of social and environmental issues, but we often face a challenge to connect these programs across our organization, so we don't prioritize it."*

My response to that would be that it is *your customers* who are demanding that companies take sustainability seriously. Certainly it can be a challenge to justify sustainability-oriented expenses to your shareholders—but in the end, the customer must have the final word on this topic or those shareholders will be left with nothing of value.

And there's a lot of demand out there. According to Euromonitor International, 61 percent of global consumers are worried about climate change and 73 percent of businesses have responded to this concern by making sustainability investments to burnish the eco-friendliness of their brands.[3]

The drive is coming from customers today. Consumers demand eco-friendly materials in their product packaging, and they want "refill" packaging that reduces waste. They want natural ingredients in their food. They want sneakers made from plastic that's been reclaimed from the ocean. They want fair trade coffee and dolphin-safe, line-caught tuna. The public is asking for all this—*really* asking for it—from the companies they support. We saw that in the assignment I worked on for that skincare brand, which I described in chapter 5. The millennial consumers we were targeting were *very* concerned that the products they use on their skin should be natural and organic.

Speaking of millennials, you've no doubt noticed how often they're referenced in this book (and others) as a desirable group to target. More than any other demographic cohort, millennials are driving this push for sustainability. Indeed, I've provided a few examples in previous chapters of data indicating that millennials admire and trust companies that undertake sustainability initiatives. Recognizing this fact—and responding to it—is an important part of following my advice in chapter 7: always seek insight from your customers.

* * *

When companies fail to think about sustainability, what happens to them? Well, when Apple launched their iPhone in 2007, they faced criticism from an environmental group called Climate Counts. This organization collects data on how companies work to reduce greenhouse gases, and they flagged Apple by including them on a list of a hundred companies that were not collecting this data and were not doing well in terms of being green.[4] This negligence of climate change was reported on NBC and MSNBC, in the *Wall Street Journal* and Reuters, and in many other mainstream news outlets at that time—and that caused serious headaches for Apple; the company had to scramble to deal with all the bad press they were suddenly getting.[5] Today the company has learned its lesson and says it plans to become carbon neutral by 2030.[6]

* * *

As consumer demand grows (i.e., as concern about climate change becomes more mainstream and increasingly fashionable), more and more companies are hopping on the bandwagon but not everyone is arriving late to the party. Some organizations have held sustainability as a value since their inception. Natura & Co (the South American corporate parent of Avon, Natura, the Beauty Shop, and Aesop) has been building sustainability efforts since the 1800s. They were the first beauty company to offer refill packaging in the beauty market in order to reduce packaging waste—a practice now emulated by everyone from Dove to Dior.[7]

Everyone now wants a piece of that sustainability action: companies such as AirVisual, IBM, and Microsoft are all developing tools to forecast air pollution in countries such as India and China. IBM has their Green Horizons Initiative, which combines machine learning and IoT to harness data from air quality stations, traffic systems, weather satellites, topographic maps, and even social media to develop predictive analytics for a two- to seven-day air pollution forecast for vulnerable cities.

In chapter 3, I mentioned how John Deere is using

technology to detect agricultural problems. The drones they use to pollinate crops are equipped with cameras and sensors that measure crop moisture, temperature, and soil composition. All this data helps to optimize production and promote healthy crops—which, of course, is good for the environment.

Patagonia encourages its employees to drive electric cars, ride bicycles, or use public transportation, and employees are actually compensated for these efforts. Their bathroom toilets are equipped with water-control sensors, and their buildings are built from recycled construction materials, with coated windows that prevent overheating. They also use solar panels for power. "Cause no harm" is built into the company's values and purpose.[8]

We also saw in chapter 5 how CNETT creates value using sustainability. CNETT focuses on sharing value to increase utilization of a product where accessing the product becomes more important than owning the product and services. This is a unique business model that exchanges resources through a platform. The company matches buyers and sellers optimizing utilization and verifies trust on their platform. CNETT ensures that transacting partners limit the counterparty verification and liability expense while reaping the benefits of sharing.

Long-term sustainability planning can create meaningful business value. For example, Unilever's ten-year Sustainable Living Plan—a business plan designed to grow Unilever's sustainability brand, drive innovation, and attract and retain talent—has doubled the company's revenue while reducing its environmental footprint. In 2018, the company announced that CEO Paul Polman had achieved a total shareholder return of 290 percent during his tenure.

So sustainability should be a starting point in everything you do.

HOW YOU CAN USE TECHNOLOGY TO DRIVE SUSTAINABILITY

I've spent the first few pages of this chapter emphasizing the importance of embracing sustainability in corporate decision-making. But the real focus of this section of the book is technology, and what I most want to get across to you is how technology drives sustainability—and makes it easy.

If your business is not a big company like Microsoft or John Deere, you may find it discouraging to read about all the audacious, *expensive* sustainability initiatives these businesses have undertaken. You may be thinking, *It's all well and good for IBM to throw its weight behind efforts to curb air pollution in Beijing, but I don't have a billion dollars at my fingertips! What can I do?*

Fortunately, there are plenty of things that you *can* do. You can tweak your product packaging or start using QR scanners to manage inventory of your merchandise better. You can encourage your employees to come to work on a bike or use public transportation (or Uber or Lyft). In this way, technology is helping many companies get to that space much faster by making life easier. And the efficiency produced by the smart use of technology translates quickly into profit!

For example, let's look at cloud computing. Companies

that implement cloud computing are going greener, whether they know it or not. A 2013 study conducted by Google found that if American businesses en masse were to move certain key software functions to the cloud—functions such as email, spreadsheets, and CRM—they would collectively cut their energy use by 87 percent. That comes to about 23 billion kilowatt hours—enough to power the city of Los Angeles for a year![9] Google also noted that despite a 550 percent increase in computer processing at its data centers between 2010 and 2018, energy consumption in that time went up by only 6 percent.[10] Amazon Web Services notes that cloud-computing data centers use less energy for cooling and other vital processes. Amazon says that it and other cloud providers are 28 percent less carbon intensive than traditional data hardware systems.[11]

Whether your business is big or small, the way you use technology can have a huge impact on environmental sustainability. Microsoft recently collaborated with Ørsted, a Danish wind technology and bioenergy provider, to design software that can analyze data from the thousands of sensors located on each of the turbines in Ørsted's ocean-based wind farms. This data—and the analysis provided by Microsoft's software—provides the company with vital insight for predictive maintenance that obviates the need for constant, enormously expensive repairs. "Each turbine is equipped with thousands of sensors and each minute, each hour, they produce vast quantities of data that we can analyze and optimize," says Ørsted CIO Michael Biermann.[12]

Ørsted is a near-perfect model for sustainable business

practices. The formerly oil-and-coal-based company has been divesting itself of those kinds of assets since 2017 and plans to be out of the coal business entirely by 2023. Indeed, Ørsted has reduced its own coal consumption by 82 percent over the last ten years,[13] and the Corporate Knights Global 100 Index has ranked them the world's most sustainable energy company three years in a row.[14]

Ørsted has also partnered with the New Jersey Institute of Technology to address the STEM education gap by supporting sustainability-oriented undergraduate scholarships and programs, such as career development opportunities in the field of offshore wind engineering.

GETTING STARTED

So what does all this look like in action?

First, you need to make sustainability a top priority; if you maximize your internal operations with sustainability technology at the earlier stages of your S-curve, you are going to become more efficient. You are going to save money, and the work you're doing will inspire your employees, making them more engaged and productive.

It doesn't matter if you don't have an exciting new sustainability vision. Feel free to try things that other companies have also tried. Experiment and do some pilot testing. Collaborate with your partners and find solutions that will benefit both of you. Utilize your data and write a hypothesis to determine how much investment you'll need to put in, what the end results should look like, and what kind of impact it will have on your business as a whole.

These kinds of projects are usually long term. They take a lot of iterations to succeed. But again, this is about improving efficiency, and it will be worth it in the long run.

Familiarizing yourself with the UN's 17 Sustainable Development Goals will give you insight into how the policy and regulatory environment in which you operate is likely to evolve over time.[15] This understanding will help you to develop more resilient business models in the future.

Above all, you need to have the CEO and senior leadership on board. When that happens, the momentum builds very quickly, and opportunities open up to drive real change in your company.

Okay, fine, you're thinking, *but where do I begin?*

You can start by examining your product and process development, using scenario planning to identify trends for PESTLED analysis. (The acronym stands for Political, Economic, Social, Technological, Legal, Environmental, and Demographic.) PESTLED is a management framework and diagnostic tool that helps you understand how external factors will affect the outcomes of business decisions. For example, *political* analysis of trends and hypothetical business decisions takes into account the effects that government policies, laws, and upcoming elections may have on your planned operations. *Economic* PESTLED analysis looks at factors like inflation, taxes, employment rates, and the health of the stock market. And so forth. In short, you go through every aspect of

PESTLED analysis, seeing each part of your company through each separate prism.

Once you've used the PESTLED framework to analyze the effect of the external environment on your business, look at your company through the lens of the ReSOLVE framework recommended by the Ellen MacArthur Foundation, a British organization dedicated to promoting a recycling-based "circular economy." ReSOLVE comprises a list of six action items a business can take to promote sustainability:

1. **R**egenerate: shift to renewable energy and materials.

2. **S**hare assets: carpool when possible; use secondhand devices.

3. **O**ptimize: increase efficiency and performance; reduce waste in production and the supply chain.

4. **L**oop: remanufacture products and components; recycle materials.

5. **V**irtualize: have conference calls on Zoom rather than in-person meetings; read e-books rather than paper books; shop online rather than in-store.

6. **E**xchange: replace old systems and products with new ones.

Companies that use the traditional ecosystem of logistics and transport are part of our environmental problem. We need to think about and to build sustainable systems in order to be part of the solution. The ReSOLVE framework can incorporate flexibility in your organization and make you more adaptable to changing environments.

* * *

Other resources that are available to drive sustainability include:

- The SDG Compass (https://sdgcompass.org), a guide for aligning your business strategies with the UN's Sustainable Development Goals (SDGs).

- Diginex solutions (https://www.diginex-solutions. com/#about-us), a "disruptive impact tech business helping organizations to address the world's most pressing ESG and sustainability issues, utilizing the latest blockchain technology to lead change and increase transparency."

- The World Economic Forum (https://www.weforum. org/), an "independent international organization committed to improving the state of the world by engaging business, political, academic and other leaders of society to shape global, regional and industry agendas."

* * *

Companies today are smarter than they used to be and should

collectively be able to come up with new ways to provide more and to give back to our society and our planet. When a business knows it has enough revenue to continue to grow, it should reorder its priorities: instead of using that money just to generate *more* revenue, that business should build sustainability initiatives.

The traditional thinking in our society is that money is the measure of success, but as the cliché goes, "money isn't everything." Business leaders should think about the values that guide them in their daily home life and bring those values to work. Applying the values that you live in your everyday life to your business allows you to become better connected with yourself and with others.

Your influence and power confer on you a responsibility to help society leverage those resources. It is important to recognize the balance between purpose and profit. These ideas are not new; adopting them is just a matter of being aware and having the consciousness to make those efforts and take those decisions.

Talk to your shareholders and think about the disconnect between their personal and professional lives: When they go home, they recycle without a second thought. But when they are in a meeting, they're not talking about recycling. Why not? Why isn't your company doing more to make the world a better, cleaner, more equitable place to live?

In Mark Lefko's 2016 book, *Global Sustainability*, Cargill CEO David MacLennan talks about how his and his family's values inform everything the company does. "It's the legacy of our founders and their descendants that they're committed to ethical business," MacLennan says. "It's just part of the family-owned shareholder culture and ethos."[16]

That's what I mean by taking your everyday values into your workplace. It's about more than just not using straws in the company cafeteria or recycling paper versus throwing it out. It is about giving back to society because someone who has the power and resources to be able to provide those things needs to do that. When you have a huge company with a lot of employees and a lot of partners, you are going to affect the environment in *some* way for good or for ill.

So what are you doing to reduce your footprint?

KEY TAKEAWAYS

- Regardless of whether *sustainability* means anything to you, you can be sure it is important to a significant portion of your customer base.

- Long-term sustainability planning can create and generate meaningful business value.

- Whether your business is big or small, the way you use technology can have a huge impact on environmental sustainability.

- Applying the values that you live in your everyday life to your business allows you to become better connected with others—including your customers.

15

LEVERAGING TECHNOLOGY TO ENGAGE YOUR CUSTOMERS AND TRANSFORM YOUR BUSINESS

Regardless of what the naysayers believe about human interaction and social media, the data show us that the abundance of technology is actually increasing the abundance of happiness all over the world.

—PETER DIAMANDIS

NOW IT'S TIME to tie together and reinforce some of the lessons you've learned in the previous chapters.

By now you understand the urgency of connecting with your customers by leveraging data to understand their needs and by offering them opportunities to collaborate. And you surely grasp the importance of an overall technology-driven strategy. By now you also realize how important it is to your future to find new channels that can be used to explore new markets and untapped market segments. And you've also seen how vital it is to your security that you cultivate long-term loyalty in your customer base: the strategies you develop and implement shouldn't just be about what you do right now; they should be designed to foster long-term growth.

In this chapter, I'll show you how implementing one of these strategies enables you to accomplish the others.

Leveraging digital technology is a great way to create awareness and solve problems for customers. Think about it for a second: What do your customers do on social media? What are they talking about? What are their complaints, and what do they love the most?

Using digital data from surveys and monitoring social media allows companies to collect Key Performance Indicators (KPIs) about customer relationships, services, products, and interactions, allowing the company to adapt and offer a personalized customer experience. Brands can reduce customer problems by identifying and monitoring them on social media. They not only acknowledge the problem or the complaint but also offer the customer a sincere apology, and they can let the customer know how they are planning to fix it so that it doesn't happen again—a promise to take corrective action gives your customer emotional reassurance.

Now let's look at some examples that demonstrate how these lessons can be applied to three different business types: small businesses, B2B companies, and B2C companies.

SMALL BUSINESSES: NANO-INFLUENCERS GET RESULTS

Since the dawn of the social media age, a lot has been written about the necessity of building relationships with social media influencers—people with large followings on Facebook, Twitter, or Instagram who can dramatically raise the profile of companies whose products they like. Some of these influencers are celebrities and some even *become* celebrities by acting as influencers.

Big brands such as Procter & Gamble use celebrity influencers when they need to generate widespread awareness quickly because most celebrities have four or five million followers. In exchange for the use of their social media platform for marketing purposes, the company will usually pay the celebrity a large fee or give them access to certain products for free.

Their services can be expensive, but cultivating relationships with influencers isn't just a game for big corporations. Smaller businesses can make excellent use of *nano-influencers*—those who have only one thousand to five thousand followers on social media. Brands typically give these nano-influencers free products or service access or pay them a small fee—which is great for a small company with a smaller budget. And the ROI is excellent: according to socialmediatoday.com, the engagement rate you can achieve by using nano-influencers is 7 percent, which is much higher than that of any other influence group.

Besides being less costly to work with, nano-influencers have active, engaged followers whom they nurture conscientiously. These influencers have a closer, more intimate relationship with their followers than macro-influencers do because the online communities in which they interact are so much smaller, and therefore they are even more trusted. Nano-influencers also tend to be more focused on niche interests or on businesses within their local area, which makes them an ideal choice for a small business that has mostly local customers.

Nano-influencers are also a great way to experiment and test out new ideas because they give you feedback. If the gist of a discussion on an influencer's social media feed is, "We didn't like this new product," then that's valuable information for you to have. Influencers benefit you not only by advocating or promoting your products but also because their activities provide real insight into how people really feel about your products or services.

Many nano-influencers are delighted to help you with your marketing efforts, and all they ask in return is to be given something for free. For example, if you're a Chinese restaurant trying to attract more customers, you can ask a nano-influencer to put pictures of your dishes on their website, Twitter account, or Facebook account, and they can advocate for you, making you visible to their five thousand followers. That is going to drive sales to your business. It's a fast and less expensive way to get marketing services when you need help—and not a bad ROI if your investment is just an occasional free bowl of chicken lo mein.

The only drawback to nano-influencers is that the brand has to create more campaigns so that they can reach a bigger set of audiences. But if you have to run a lot of campaigns, you can use multiple nano-influencers. You might have up to twenty or thirty nano-influencers talking about your new promotion at the same time. Think about it: if thirty nano-influencers are willing to help you and they have five thousand followers each, well, just do the math!

So what kinds of influencers do you need and how do you find them? The answer to that depends on a number of other questions: What are your goals? What are you trying to do with your messaging, and who are you trying to reach? How many people do you need to reach in order to achieve your goals? Once you establish these, you will know what kind of influencer you can use to reach the market.

The way you identify these influencers is simple: you search for them on various social media platforms—especially Instagram and Facebook (now known as Meta). Look for someone who has a lot of followers. You want to see that they have nurtured this group of followers and that these followers are consistent. You can type in keywords to find them; for example, if you are in the beauty industry and are looking for a nano-influencer, you should search Instagram for content about beauty and take note of anybody who is talking about beauty and has the requisite number of followers.

Be sure to scroll through the influencer's posts with a few key questions in mind: Is this person the right fit for you? What kinds of things are they talking about? Are they respectful with their followers? Do they engage with them? Are they consistent in posting? Do people have good feedback about them? You can learn all of that just by doing keyword searches. After you've determined that an influencer is suitable, set up a call with them and see if they are willing to help you by advocating for your products or your campaign. Be sure to tell them up front what you will do for them in exchange for their services.

I want those of you who run small businesses to know that you can do this because the big companies are already doing it. Bigger companies can use nano-influencers just as effectively, and they do. Gillette, for example, used nano-influencers to raise awareness for the launch of their new Venus razor. Procter & Gamble uses influencers, too, as do L'Oréal and Clorox. Unilever uses influencers at all levels, including nano-influencers, to build awareness and create trust and credibility for their brands. The Dove Real Beauty campaign, which was launched in 2004, is still using influencers after all these years—especially nano-influencers—to build long-term engagement and brand loyalty.

Companies need to maintain an online presence and make it part of their operational cost, not just a marketing cost. Many companies focus on advertising and engagement messages just to nudge the customers who are already on their way to purchasing their products or services. But this expenditure only pays for harvesting the current market—it does not drive future sales. Companies need to think about long-term engagement strategies that use integrated marketing communication frameworks and connect to the company's purpose.

B2B BUSINESSES: IN ORDER TO TRANSFORM, MAERSK MAKES A FILM

The pandemic has changed the landscape for B2B companies, many of which will have to revise their businesses to build better connections with their customers and to focus more on digital strategies and customer experience. We've seen many B2B businesses struggle during the pandemic to connect with their partners and customers online when they were no longer able to send their sales reps out to do that work in person. This is a new environment for them, and they need to work on generating emotional resonance rather than focus exclusively on their value propositions.

Let me tell you about Maersk, the gigantic ocean shipping company that has been around for 130 years. In 2019, Maersk was struggling. The company controls 18 percent of the ocean shipping market and has relationships with the world's largest brands, but they're seeking to transform themselves from a firm known just as an ocean shipping company to one that is globally recognized as a full logistic services company. To do this, Maersk knew they needed to get the attention of their customers—not an easy task because there is already a strong perception in the market of who they are: they dominate the ocean shipping market, but no one thinks of them in the context of ground logistics.

What they needed was to create new communications messaging to announce their new direction as a full-service logistics company—so they did something bold. They made a film to connect with their audience.[1] The film was only about five minutes long, but it was emotional and captivating.

Maersk used integrated new web services as well as print, banner, webinar, and public relations campaigns to make the announcement. The result: the film got more online views than Marvel's *Avengers: Endgame* trailer. Brent Nelson, chief strategy officer for the Leo Burnett advertising agency, said that they were basically using a B2C marketing mindset when they created the film, looking at different segments of C-suite decision-makers and determining what key drivers they used when making decisions and picking partners. And it worked: their campaign generated a 24 percent increase in logistics and services revenue.

Maersk used customer insight and demonstrated a deep understanding of their intangible assets: their knowledge of the industry, customer lists, major contracts, and their experienced management team. Maersk is an industry leader in ocean shipping logistics, they have long-term global partnership capability, and they have a technology-driven capability to address all kinds of logistics solutions. If we were to examine these capabilities on a deeper level and how they combined them to create this campaign, we would find that they used *predictive* capabilities.

Leaning into those capabilities, Maersk devised a message that would grab the attention of the C-suite of any potential new customer. This 130-year-old shipping company transformed itself to expand to new service offerings, to open new opportunities for

Horizon Two and Horizon Three projects, and to use technology-driven solutions to integrate their logistics solutions.

In short, Maersk's corporate leadership exhibited the entrepreneurial trait of deep curiosity and used cross-fertilization of different domains and markets to select their best ideas. Maersk understood how to identify their differentiating capabilities and integrate them. They were comfortable standing apart from the rest of the B2B industry by breaking the norm. They wanted their teams and stakeholders to believe the impossible.

For leaders, the takeaway from the Maersk example is this: Companies can shape their future by extending their capabilities to confront change and become more adaptable. They can leverage existing customer relationships to meet their known needs today *and* the unknown needs of tomorrow. They can be bold enough to step out of their industry, to realign it around their core strengths. They can use their leadership position to reshape the category by developing mass marketing capabilities that provide a high level of influence. Maersk tied their new strategies to their purpose of connecting the world.

By the way, you don't need a fancy film crew or a big budget; a creative development site called Tongal makes it possible to create a TV or Internet ad in just a few weeks.

B2C BUSINESSES: ALDI CHANGES NEGATIVE PERCEPTIONS— BY EMBRACING THEM

Aldi is a globally known grocery store chain headquartered in Germany but with stores all over Europe, Australia, and the

United States. Aldi has always been very popular in Germany; Germans love the low-key store environment and the low prices, and they love Aldi's down-to-earth image.

But when Aldi opened in the United Kingdom in 1990, they struggled to connect with the British public. Curiously, the very basic things the German public loves about Aldi—it's *very* inexpensive, and the stores have a simple, unpretentious atmosphere—stigmatized it in Britain. Britons perceived the stores as shabby and too small, with no big-name brands on the shelves, and saw Aldi as a purveyor of cheap, poor-quality food and goods. British schoolboys would taunt one another by jeering, "Yer mum shops at Aldi!"

Aldi in the United Kingdom was seen as a place for low-income families, and the brand was struggling to stay relevant against big competitors such as Tesco. They had less than a 2 percent market share, but their goal was to become one of the top five grocery retailers in the UK market by 2020.

In the early 2010s, Aldi decided to respond boldly to their image problem by embracing it. They built campaigns such as *Like Brand* and *Swap & Save*, driving home the message that Aldi's products are every bit as good as their competitors' goods—but they're cheaper. For example, one very funny and hugely popular *Like Brand* ad shows an elderly woman—a "grandma" type—holding two boxes of tea: one box is labeled £3.00 ("I buy this tea for my husband; he likes tea.") and the other is only £1.99 ("He also likes this one."). After looking into the camera for a moment, she says, matter-of-factly, "I don't like tea. I like gin."[2]

248

This message is reinforced by the *Swap & Save* ads, which invite the viewer to "swap" their expensive favorite store for the cheaper (but just as good!) option of Aldi's. Together these ad campaigns drive home the point that there's no shame in saving money by shopping at Aldi if what you're buying is just as good as the fancier, more expensive stuff you can get elsewhere. The goal was to establish parity of quality and focus on how much consumers can save by shopping there. Aldi, the ads proclaimed, is a brand of low-cost products from a high-quality grocer.

Aldi's business model now is to differentiate themselves as a deep-discount grocery store—deeper than Walmart, deeper than Giant, deeper than any other store out there. This is evident the moment you walk into an Aldi store: there is a *blah* kind of feeling. No emotion is triggered by the store's drab appearance. You just go in and purchase what you need, then leave. They don't even have grocery bags; you have to bring your own bags, and you have to put a quarter into a locking device in order to obtain a grocery cart.

The entire purpose of this no-frills environment is to save the customer money, and that purpose is reflected in every aspect of the design model. The way their shelving is built, the casual way products are placed throughout the store—every single piece of the experience is discounted, a cost-saving for the store, and that discount is passed on to the customer. They do sell a few name brands, but most of what you'll find on their shelves is the Aldi brand or a no-name generic brand. Their business model is the exact opposite of the Amazon Go model, where every time you pick up a sandwich from the shelf, monitors and sensors let the company know and you are charged for it. Aldi presents themselves as an old-school grocery store that is just trying to save everyone money, and they don't need conspicuous technology to maintain this image—but when it comes to advertising, they know what they're doing.

To transform their stores and achieve their goal—to become a top-five grocery retailer in the United Kingdom—Aldi went back to the core philosophy first articulated by cofounder Karl Albrecht: "Aldi does not ask how much they can charge for a product; they ask how little they can sell it for."

The challenge for Aldi was to persuade their UK shoppers that these distinctive features—smaller stores, no fancy brands, and prices so low that even poor people can afford them—are features, not drawbacks. They needed to make them understand that Aldi's products are just as good as Tesco's—hence the *Like Brands* and *Swap & Save* campaigns and the subsequent introduction of Aldi's perennial Christmastime mascot, Kevin the Carrot. Kevin is deployed every year to remind the public that Aldi's produce is fresh from local farms and is just as good as what you'll find at Whole Foods or anywhere else—only much less expensive. Aldi imbues their campaigns with humor, features "real" people rather than good-looking actors, and makes use of all possible touchpoints—social media (especially Twitter and Facebook), news outlets, radio and TV, and so on—to reach their UK audience.

So how successful have these campaigns been over the past ten years? Social media engagement data indicates they've reached over 109,000 members, and those people put up more than thirty-five posts per day on Aldi's Facebook (Meta) page. In 2010, when this long-term strategy was conceived, Aldi held 2 percent of the retail grocery store market, and by 2019 they were at 7.9 percent, a 295 percent increase in growth. A supermarket that middle-class (and even some working-class) people had always avoided has now become a widely accepted and even beloved institution in the United Kingdom.

* * *

I picked Aldi as an example because I wanted to show that when you are creating a customer engagement or experience marketing effort, you can't just do it for today; you *have* to do it for the long term and you *have* to differentiate yourself. Aldi may still be focused primarily on a niche market (although these campaigns have clearly expanded their market share), but that is fine, as long as the company survives. The first goal of any business is that the company must not die!

Aldi certainly isn't dying; their stores are all over Europe and the company has come to the United States, where they hope to have 2,500 stores by the end of 2022.[3] Obviously, they must be doing something right.

And they are very ambitious—remember, they want to be one of the top five grocers in the United Kingdom, competing with stores such as the more upscale Tesco, which is a dominant giant in that market.

So how do you compete with the big guys? First, by not competing with them on their own terms—at least not yet.

Second, you need to implement long-term strategies in lieu of short-term tactics. Aldi and Maersk are not merely employing customer engagement using their digital capabilities; they are building strategies for the future—which is what everyone should be doing. Don't ever do anything just for today because that ROI is not going to last long. It is going to be miniscule in the long run compared to what you can achieve over the next few years if you stick to it. Companies need to focus on fostering long-term growth and in building deep, long-term loyalty connections with their customers.

How are you using technology to focus on social ROI? How are you using engagement and experiences to build brand awareness, transform your company, and ensure long-term customer loyalty? You need to focus not only on solving customer problems and creating awareness but also on creating magical experiences and coming up with new ideas and services that you can offer to the market. Remember this: the better a company understands and improves its capabilities, and the more it interacts with its customers and learns about them, the better its management will understand how to ensure long-term growth.

To create transformation, leaders need vision and need to see digital technology as an opportunity to create better customer experiences and drive engagement. Developing your digital capabilities will make you more flexible, which will help you reach more audiences locally as well as globally—and this will drive stronger revenues. Collecting and examining data will enable you to identify new opportunities. Together, these behaviors will create efficiencies in your operations, leverage your existing assets, and reinforce engagement strategies with your customers.

KEY TAKEAWAYS

- It's imperative to use and incorporate customer feedback to explore new avenues for long-term growth strategies.

- B2B companies can reinvent advertising by leveraging digital technology to create awareness and solve problems for customers.

- Start small with nano-influencers in order to achieve results.

- Companies can shape their future by extending their capabilities to confront change and become more adaptable.

FINAL THOUGHTS

Struggle is a necessary component of success.

—The 3M Company[1]

NO INDUSTRY IS IMMUNE to disruption, and the disruptions that are coming may be every bit as severe as those we saw during the COVID-19 pandemic. Business leaders must learn to embrace new perspectives if they want to remain successful and realize their full potential.

The pandemic drove a great many businesses into bankruptcy, and many more struggled with considerable loss of revenue. The ones that survived are still trying to pick up the pieces, but many industries are still struggling, especially health care, financial services, education, transportation, energy production and distribution, real estate, insurance, manufacturing, and legal services. Companies need to learn how to adapt better and how to innovate—in fact, innovation should be at the top of everyone's list of priorities, regardless of whether you are a large, midsize, or small company.

According to *Harvard Business Review*, when digital disruption occurred in 2000, some 52 percent of Fortune 500 companies went bankrupt, were acquired, or ceased to exist.[2] The consequences of the financial disruption in 2008 were likewise catastrophic, and I'm sure I don't need to remind you how economically devastating the pandemic has been. Whatever external disruption is going to happen next, everyone is likely to be affected—so everyone needs to be prepared to weather the storm. Today the lifespan of a Fortune 500 company is predicted to be fewer than fifteen years.[3]

We know for a fact that a great many disruptive technologies are coming—some of them are already here. Technology disruption happened in 2000, and it is going to happen again soon. Indeed, it is already happening. AI is now being used in ways that no one would have thought possible a decade ago. Quantum computing, which is a new form of technology disruption, is now happening more quickly than anyone could ever have imagined, enabling breakthroughs in health care (such as gene sequencing and development of new drugs) and disrupting financial markets with faster, more accurate market projections. Companies that can keep up with market trends and new technology disruption will have at least a chance of survival—and I'm sure I don't need to tell you what will become of those that can't keep up with those trends.

Reskilling the workforce is going to be an urgent necessity in the near future, which is why (now) President Biden suggested that coal miners should transition to the jobs of the future by learning to code. Regardless of your political position, it is the job of government and private enterprise alike to think about the future, so it's prudent to take notice when governments start talking about whether we are going to be able to protect entire industries.

Also, we can't ignore the financial technology disruption that is also under way, portending big changes in personal finances, insurance, banking, lending industries, capital markets, and even the way we do payments. When I'm shopping online, I have the option to use Amazon Pay on any website. When I check out and I see an Amazon Pay tab, I click on it, and it knows where I live, it knows my credit card number, and with one click I'm checked out. Our lives are getting simpler and simpler by the day, changing the way we pay for items we buy online.

SUSTAINABILITY

When President Biden was elected, the United States rejoined the Paris Agreement. Again, it doesn't matter what you think of Joe Biden—the writing is now on the wall for any company that doesn't prioritize environmental and ethical sustainability.

This is not just a matter of increased regulatory scrutiny (although, for all we know, a tighter regulatory regime may very well be coming within the next four years); it's a matter of what consumers—especially the valuable millennial demographic—are increasingly going to demand. If you ignore them, they'll want to know why you're not doing anything to help the environment. They get excited when Nike says, "We made this shoe out of plastic that we reclaimed from the ocean!" In short, consumers demand sustainability, so if you want to make money, you need to be on board. It should be part of your mission, part of who you are.

Moreover, you need to see the upside: you will make longer-term profits.

One of the most useful services we provide aligns companies' initiatives with specific United Nations Sustainable Developmental Goals (SDGs). When we work with clients, we make sure that we're aligning these sustainable development goals with *their* strategies. We create your SDG-aligned strategy in such a way that it delivers for you—and as a bonus, you are helping the planet at the same time.

A CAPABILITY-DRIVEN STRATEGY

A capability-driven strategy is critical for success. Remember, to create market value, companies first have to get noticed and break through a lot of noise. You therefore need to understand how to build and use your capabilities more effectively to drive new growth, reach new markets, cut costs, and achieve more profit. Companies should realize the importance of a technology strategy that creates efficiency and reinforces and complements their other capabilities. Typically, the missing piece here is that capabilities are not aligned, which leads to a failure to utilize resources properly.

CULTURE

An organization that has a diverse and inclusive culture can benefit your company in critical decision-making situations and help you achieve greater flexibility and alignment across divisions. When a culture is aligned and everyone has a shared purpose, the company can quickly respond to change when necessary.

Diversity is important not only for your employees but for C-suite business leaders. As we saw in the Domino's example of a board member with expertise in technology, if you surround yourself with individuals who have different expertise and backgrounds, you'll benefit from their different perceptions and insights.

To stay ahead of trends and understand external changes, business leaders should attend university lectures and conferences in cross-sectors. They should prioritize developing fresh perspectives and expose themselves to new surroundings to challenge their thinking. It's not enough to just build communities inside the workplace; as business leaders, you need to build communities and strong connections *outside of work*.

INNOVATION: INCREMENTAL AND RADICAL

Innovation is often misunderstood. Let me explain.

A street vendor has less complexity than an organization, and therefore when she approaches a new idea, she doesn't feel awkward about trying it. She has patience and is forward-looking. Unfortunately, too many companies commonly overlook new ideas or fail to pursue them because they feel awkward and uncertain. So how do you reduce that uncertainty? You put your project under a spotlight, write hypotheses, test, and experiment. If you don't take the idea to the experimentation phase, you will never collect enough data to reduce your risk.

* * *

This book focuses on many different capabilities—channel, process, customer insight, technology, customer experience and engagement, collaboration, and co-creation—and identifies ways to improve those capabilities. But there are other capabilities that can help you strengthen your company.

The important thing to remember is *alignment* in everything you do and every decision you take. Also remember that people are buying your products and services, whether B2B or B2C, to enrich their lives. Customer insight and scenario planning are therefore critical foundational factors for decision-makers who have to establish projections based on these assumptions. Today in the post-COVID world, companies need to have flexibility, resilience, and speed to gain market advantages. They have to be ready to take calculated risks, have a culture of innovation, and be proactive in making strategic moves. Business leaders need to develop an adaptability muscle, focus on *why* they're doing their work, and be able to recognize when they are in a default mindset.

FINAL THOUGHTS

* * *

It is important to make innovation a priority, and that starts with an entrepreneurial mindset—thinking big and bold, with a long-term vision, unafraid to take risks and sail fast.

Companies shouldn't settle for efforts and wins in just one horizon. They should think bigger and longer term. They should focus on all three horizons simultaneously. This is where ideas can cross-pollinate and you can start to build momentum for your company.

I want to stress that I don't think enough companies are working with three horizons simultaneously, and that is something they need to be doing. That's because we live in a market in which rapid changes are constantly happening.

The speed at which companies learn and use their learning can spell the difference between survival and failure. Your future may soon depend on your ability to be just as flexible and adaptable as a street vendor.

And I know a little something about that.

NOTES

AN INVITATION

1. Robin Sharma, *The World Changer's Manifesto* (Lucerne, Switzerland: Titan Academy Global, 2019), 130.

CHAPTER 1: THINK LIKE A STREET VENDOR

1. Peter Drucker, *Innovation and Entrepreneurship: Practice and Principles* (New York: Harper & Row, 1985).
2. "3M History," 3M, accessed September 10, 2021, https://www.3m.com/3M/en_US/company-us/about-3m/history/.
3. Mark Reilly, "Safety Sells for 3M, but Not Post-Its, So the Company Plans Cost Cuts," *Minneapolis/St. Paul Business Journal*, April 28, 2020, https://www.bizjournals.com/twincities/news/2020/04/28/safety-sells-for-3m-but-not-post-its-so-the.html.
4. Reilly, "Safety Sells for 3M."
5. "A Q&A with 3M's New CEO Mike Roman," 3M, accessed September 10, 2021, https://news.3m.com/A-Q-A-with-3Ms-New-CEO-Mike-Roman.
6. *A Century of Innovation: The 3M Story* (Maplewood, MN: 3M Company, 2002), 21.
7. 3M Company, *Century of Innovation*, 19.
8. Vanessa Gomes, "Malaysia's Standing in International Supply Chain in Jeopardy," *The Edge Markets*, March 27, 2020, https://www.theedgemarkets.com/article/malaysias-standing-international-supply-chain-jeopardy.

CHAPTER 2: BUILDING BRIDGES TO LUCRATIVE UNTAPPED MARKET SEGMENTS

1. Seth Godin, *This Is Marketing: You Can't Be Seen until You Learn to See* (New York: Penguin, 2018).
2. Jonah Berger, "How to Trigger Word of Mouth," *Jonah's Blog*, accessed August 12, 2021, https://jonahberger.com/how-to-trigger-word-of-mouth/.
3. Dr. Pete Etchells, "Why Are So Many People Playing *Animal Crossing*?," *Science Focus*, June 29, 2020, https://www.sciencefocus.com/news/why-are-so-many-people-playing-animal-crossing/.
4. "Why Robin Sharma Is a Leader to Leaders," https://www.robinsharma.com/course/personal-mastery-academy-online.
5. David Ridley, "J&J's Nicorette QuickMist SmartTrack—Getting Inside One of 2020's Biggest UK Launches," HBW Insight, February 24, 2021, https://hbw.pharmaintelligence.informa.com/RS151046/JJs-Nicorette-QuickMist-SmartTrack--Getting-Inside-One-Of-2020s-Biggest-UK-Launches.
6. pradagroup.com/news-media-section.
7. "Dove | Courage is Beautiful," Dove US, April 8, 2020, https://www.youtube.com/watch?v=sQOq0-ODBbc.

CHAPTER 3: SUBSCRIPTION MODELS AND THE "INTERNET OF THINGS"

1. Clayton Christensen, "Disruptive Technologies and Disruptive Innovations," Big Think, https://bigthink.com/videos/disruptive-technologies-and-disruptive-innovations/.
2. "About Subscribe and Save," Amazon, accessed March 29, 2021, https://www.amazon.com/b/

ref=s9_acss_bw_cg_test_1a1_w?&node=15283820011&pf_rd_m=ATVPDKIKX0DER&pf_
rd_s=merchandised-search-4&pf_rd_r=5NZ5VPQ7V90CYTA4Q17J&pf_rd_t=101&pf_rd_
p=37db1d38-f7c4-4715-a7aa-e9cb866813e9&pf_rd_i=5856181011.

3. Jacob Morgan, "A Simple Explanation of 'The Internet of Things,'" *Forbes*, May 13, 2014, https://
    www.forbes.com/sites/jacobmorgan/2014/05/13/simple-explanation-internet-things-that-
    anyone-can-understand/?sh=7ccf34251d09.

4. "Smart Fridge," Samsung, https://www.samsung.com/us/explore/family-hub-refrigerator/overview/.

5. "John Deere Turns to IoT to Make Smart Farming a Reality," Internet of Business, accessed
    March 29, 2021, https://internetofbusiness.com/john-deere-turns-iot-smart-farming/.

6. "Here's How John Deere Is Working with Farmers to Improve Agriculture," Field Service USA,
    accessed March 31, 2021, https://fieldserviceusa.wbresearch.com/john-deere-farmers-
    improve-agriculture-strategy-ty-u.

CHAPTER 4: EXPLORING NEW MARKETS

1. Philip Kotler, *Marketing Management* 15th Ed. (Boston: Pearson, 2016).

2. Verne Harnish, *The Greatest Business Decisions of All Time* (New York: Time Home Entertainment, 2012).

3. Sean Peek, "Could a Startup Incubator Benefit Your Business?," US Chamber of Commerce,
    accessed April 6, 2021, https://www.uschamber.com/co/run/business-financing/startup-incubator.

4. Samantha Conti, "Unilever's Sunny Jain Lays Out His Strategic Vision," *Women's Wear Daily*,
    December 10, 2020, https://wwd.com/beauty-industry-news/beauty-features/unilevers-sunny-
    jain-lays-out-his-strategic-vision-1234661784/.

5. Conti, "Unilever's Sunny Jain."

6. "Watch Out for Isha Insight 2021," Isha Insight, https://www.ishaeducation.org/insight/.

7. Saritha Rai, "Twitter Acquires India-Based 'Missed Call' Startup ZipDial," *Forbes*, January 20,
    2015, https://www.forbes.com/sites/saritharai/2015/01/20/twitter-acquires-india-based-missed-call-
    firm-zipdial/?sh=5487e55d7115.

8. Saritha Rai, "Why Twitter Bought Bangalore 'Missed Call' Startup ZipDial," *Forbes Asia*, January
    28, 2015, https://www.forbes.com/sites/saritharai/2015/01/28/where-140-characters-is-a-luxury
    /?sh=34b901432b6b.

9. Rai, "Twitter Acquires."

10. "10 Successful American Businesses That Have Failed Overseas," International Business Degree Guide,
    https://internationalbusinessguide.org/10-successful-american-businesses-that-have-failed-overseas/.

CHAPTER 5: FINDING NEW CHANNELS AND INCREASING EFFICIENCY

1. Peter Drucker, *The Practice of Management* (New York: Harper & Row, 1954).

2. "1995: The Calm Before the Storm?," *Next Generation*, January 1996; Jonathan Chew, "Microsoft
    Launched This Product 20 Years Ago and Changed the World," *Fortune*, August 24, 2015, https://
    fortune.com/2015/08/24/20-years-microsoft-windows-95/.

3. Bella Rushi, "Channel Development: Connect Better with Customers," Symmetri Consulting, October
    19, 2021, https://symmetriconsulting.com/channel-development-connect-better-with- customers/.

CHAPTER 6: WHEN YOU'RE NOT INNOVATING ENOUGH—AND WHAT TO DO ABOUT IT

1. Jason L. Riley, "Was the $5 Billion Worth It? A decade into his record-breaking education philan-
    thropy, Bill Gates talks teachers, charters—and regrets," *Wall Street Journal*, July 23, 2011, https://
    www.wsj.com/articles/SB10001424053111903554904576461571362279948.

2. PricewaterhouseCoopers, "The Global Innovation 1,000 Study," accessed April 19, 2021, https://www.strategyand.pwc.com/gx/en/insights/innovation1000.html.

3. Gabriel Madway, "Blockbuster Withdraws Proposal to Acquire Circuit City," *Forbes*, July 2008, https://web.archive.org/web/20080705151450/http://www.forbes.com/afxnewslimited/feeds/afx/2008/07/01/afx5175198.html.

4. David Marin, "The Amazon Fire Phone Failure," Slidebean, July 30, 2020, https://slidebean.com/blog/startups-amazon-fire.

5. Magnus Penker and S. B. Khoh, "Cultivating Growth and Radical Innovation Success in the Fourth Industrial Revolution with Big Data Analytics," 2018 IEEE International Conference on Industrial Engineering and Engineering Management, https://www.semanticscholar.org/paper/Cultivating-Growth-and-Radical-Innovation-Success-Penker-Khoh/eb53703299a361c1e250c9f-95c5a27dce4fae06b

6. Matthew Boyle, "Questions for . . . Reed Hastings," *Fortune*, May 23, 2007, https://money.cnn.com/magazines/fortune/fortune_archive/2007/05/28/100034248/.

7. Imani Moise, David Henry, and Noor Zainab Hussain, "Bank of America Eyes Loan Growth After First Decline in Six Years," Reuters, January 19, 2021, https://www.reuters.com/article/us-bank-of-america-results-idUSKBN29O1BU.

8. Jim Collins and Jerry I. Porras, *Built to Last: Successful Habits of Visionary Companies* (New York: HarperBusiness, 1994).

CHAPTER 7: STALK YOUR CUSTOMERS: OBTAINING CUSTOMER INSIGHTS

1. Bill Gates, *Business at the Speed of Thought: Using a Digital Nervous System* (New York: Warner Books, 1999).

2. "Cascade Platinum Products," Cascade, accessed April 28, 2021, https://cascadeclean.com/en-us/products/by-line/platinum/;"Our Purpose," HSBC, accessed April 28, 2021, https://www.hsbc.com/who-we-are/purpose-values-and-strategy.

3. HSBC Group, "Our Purpose," accessed February 4, 2022, https://www.hsbc.com/who-we-are/purpose-values-and-strategy.

4. "Priority Earth: Our Initiative to Deliver a More Sustainable Future," FedEx, accessed April 28, 2021, https://www.fedex.com/en-us/sustainability.html.

CHAPTER 8: CHOOSING THE RIGHT COLLABORATION PARTNERS

1. Patrick Moorehead, "Why I'm Not Surprised That IBM and Intel Are Collaborating on Chip Tech," *Forbes*, April 15, 2021, https://www.forbes.com/sites/patrickmoorehead/2021/04/15/why-im-not-surprised-that-ibm-and-intel-are-collaborating-chip-tech/?sh=5088430c10a9.

2. John LaMattina, "Universities Stepping Up Efforts to Discover Drugs," *Forbes*, October 21, 2013, https://www.forbes.com/sites/johnlamattina/2013/10/21/universities-stepping-up-efforts-to-discover-drugs/?sh=5088ffa722f2.

3. LaMattina, "Universities Stepping Up Efforts."

4. David Shaywitz, "The Startling History Behind Merck's New Cancer Blockbuster," *Forbes*, July 26, 2017, https://www.forbes.com/sites/davidshaywitz/2017/07/26/the-startling-history-behind-mercks-new-cancer-blockbuster/?sh=33e9b84d948d.

5. Alex Keown, "Keytruda Set to Become World's Top-Selling Drug, Forecast Shows," *Biospace*, October 4, 2019, https://www.biospace.com/article/keytruda-set-to-become-world-s-top-selling-drug-forecast-shows/.

6. Alexis Fournier, "Customer Co-creation Examples: 10 Companies Doing It Right," *Braineet*, March

20, 2019, https://www.braineet.com/blog/co-creation-examples/#dhl.

7. Paddy Miller and Thomas Wedell-Wedellsborg. *Innovation as Usual: How to Help Your People Bring Great Ideas to Life.* (Boston: Harvard Business Review Press, 2013)

CHAPTER 9: CO-CREATING WITH YOUR CUSTOMERS

1. Adrian Howard, "Faster Horses," *Adrian Howard* (blog), September 9, 2019, https://medium.com/@adrianh/faster-horses-50ff8bb1bb62.

2. Patrick Vlaskovits, "Henry Ford, Innovation, and That 'Faster Horse' Quote," *Harvard Business Review*, August 29, 2011, https://hbr.org/2011/08/henry-ford-never-said-the-fast.

3. "Nike and Google Create Global Online Community for Football," Nike News, March 20, 2006, accessed May 21, 2021, https://news.nike.com/news/nike-and-google-create-global-online-community-for-football.

4. Geraldine E. Willigan, "High-Performance Marketing: An Interview with Nike's Phil Knight," *Harvard Business Review*, July–August 1992, https://hbr.org/1992/07/high-performance-marketing-an-interview-with-nikes-phil-knight.

5. Madanmohan Rao, "The Co-creation Canvas: How to Innovate with Customers and Business Partners," YourStory, February 5, 2019, https://yourstory.com/2019/02/co-creation-canvas-customer-engagement/amp.

CHAPTER 10: RIDING THE S-CURVE: DEVELOPING NEW EXPERTISE AND NEW IDEAS

1. Magnus Penker, "Want to Keep Growing Your Business? Radical Innovation Is the Safest Way to Go," *Inc.*, March/April 2021, https://www.inc.com/magazine/202104/magnus-penker/s-curve-radical-innovation-ideas.html.

2. "The Innovation Horizons Introduction 4," Innovation 360, October 22, 2018, YouTube, https://www.youtube.com/watch?v=jWHE5VWnwi0.

3. Stephen Coley, Mehrdad Baghai, and David White, *The Alchemy of Growth* (London: Orion Business Books, 1999).

4. "Enduring Ideas: The Three Horizons of Growth," McKinsey & Company, December 1, 2009, https://www.mckinsey.com/business-functions/strategy-and-corporate-finance/our-insights/enduring- ideas-the-three-horizons-of-growth.

5. "Enduring Ideas."

6. Shigetaka Komori, *Innovating Out of Crisis: How Fujifilm Survived (and Thrived) As Its Core Business Was Vanishing* (Berkeley, CA: Stone Bridge Press, 2015).

7. *Innovating Out of Crisis.*

8. "Moonshot Projects with John Saiz," *Play Bold* podcast, Innovation 360, https://innovation360.com/play-bold-moonshot-projects-with-john-saiz/.

CHAPTER 11: OVERCOMING YOUR FEARS ABOUT BUSINESS TECHNOLOGY

1. Ed Addison and Shahar Keinan, "Cloud Computing: Using Quantum Molecular Design & Cloud Computing to Improve the Accuracy & Success Probability of Drug Discovery," *Drug Development & Delivery*, March 2016, https://drug-dev.com/cloud-computing-using-quantum-molecular-design-cloud-computing-to-improve-the-accuracy-success-probability-of-drug-discovery/.

2. "Cloud Pharmaceuticals Wins U.S.-China Health Innovation Competition," Cloud Pharmaceuticals, October 24, 2018, http://www.cloudpharmaceuticals.com/aipharma-825628-354706-885940-629729-963306.html.

NOTES

CHAPTER 12: HIRE A CTO: WHY YOU MUST SOLVE YOUR TECHNOLOGY CHALLENGES IN-HOUSE

1. Bill Campbell, *Trillion Dollar Coach: The Leadership Playbook of Silicon Valley's* (New York: Harper Business, 2019). Bill Campbell (1940–2016) was the board director for Apple Inc. and CEO of Intuit, and in the course of his career he coached many business luminaries, including Steve Jobs, Jeff Bezos, and Jack Dorsey.

2. Alicia Kelso, "How Becoming 'a Tech Company That Sells Pizza' Delivered Huge for Domino's," *Forbes*, April 30, 2018, https://www.forbes.com/sites/aliciakelso/2018/04/30/delivery-digital-provide-dominos-with-game-changing-advantages/?sh=737301fa7771; "Domino's Pizza CEO: 'We're Investing Aggressively' in Driverless Cars, Timeline of 3-5 Years," *Mad Money with Jim Cramer*, CNBC, March 5, 2018, https://www.cnbc.com/video/2018/03/05/dominos-pizza-ceo-were- investing-aggressively-in-driverless-cars.html.

3. "Biography, C. Andrew Ballard," Domino's, accessed July 7, 2021, https://ir.dominos.com/board-member/c-andrew-ballard.

CHAPTER 13: USING TECHNOLOGY TO STAY AHEAD OF YOUR COMPETITORS

1. Robert Reiss, "Leadership Quotes from 10 Transformative CEOs During 2020," *Forbes*, December 1, 2020, https://www.forbes.com/sites/robertreiss/2020/12/01/leadership-quotes-from-10-transformative-ceos-during-2020/?sh=304be40c24f4.

2. "Computers That Smell: Intel's Neuromorphic Chip Can Sniff Out Hazardous Chemicals," Intel, March 16, 2020, https://newsroom.intel.com/news/computers-smell-intels-neuromorphic-chip-sniff-hazardous-chemicals/#gs.6h4zki.

3. "Neuromorphic Computing: Beyond Today's AI," Intel, accessed July 15, 2021, https://www.intel.com/content/www/us/en/research/neuromorphic-computing.html.

4. "Amazon Go," accessed July 15, 2021, https://www.amazon.com/b?ie=UTF8&node=16008589011.

5. Jeffrey Dastin, "Amazon Launches Business Selling Automated Checkout to Retailers," Reuters, March 9, 2020, https://www.reuters.com/article/us-amazon-com-store-technology/amazon-launches-business-selling-automated-checkout-to-retailers-idUSKBN20W0OD.

6. "What Science Says About Food," Science Says, https://www.thesciencesays.com.

7. Geoffrey A. Moore, *Crossing the Chasm* (New York: Harper Business Essentials, 1991); Malcolm Gladwell, *The Tipping Point* (New York: Little, Brown, 2000).

CHAPTER 14: USING TECH TO DRIVE SUSTAINABILITY

1. Antonio Guterres, "Remarks to Informal Meeting of the General Assembly on the Independent High-Level Panel on Digital Cooperation," United Nations, June 10, 2019, https://www.un.org/sg/en/content/sg/speeches/2019-06-10/independent-high-level-panel-digital-cooperation-remarks-general-assembly.

2. V. Kasturi Rangan, Lisa Chase, and Sohel Karim, "The Truth About CSR," *Harvard Business Review*, January/February 2015, https://hbr.org/2015/01/the-truth-about-csr.

3. Maria Coronado Robles, "From Sustainability to Purpose Q&A: Awareness, Communication and Investment," Euromonitor International, January 20, 2021, https://blog.euromonitor.com/from-sustainability-to-purpose-qa-awareness-communication-and-investment/.

4. Adrian Kingsley-Hughes, "Climate Counts Tells Climate-Conscious Buyers to Avoid Apple," *ZD Net*, May 9, 2008, https://www.zdnet.com/article/climate-counts-tells-climate-conscious-buyers-to-avoid-apple/.

5. Chris Foresman, "Climate Counts: Apple Lags on Climate Change Policy," *Ars Technica*, April 9, 2008, https://arstechnica.com/gadgets/2008/05/climate-counts-apple-lags-on-climate-change-policy/.

6. Kim Lyons, "Apple Launches $200 Million Fund for Climate Change," The Verge, April 15, 2021 https://www.theverge.com/2021/4/15/22385552/apple-200-million-fund-climate-change-environment.

7. Marci Robin, "23 Refillable Products to Try for a Less Wasteful Beauty Regimen," *Allure*, April 4, 2021, https://www.allure.com/gallery/refillable-beauty-products.

8. "Patagonia's Balancing Act: Chasing Mass-Market Appeal While Doing No Harm," *Retailing Management*, October 10, 2016, https://www.theretailingmanagement.com/?p=1341.

9. Ucilia Wang, "A Google-Funded Study Quantifies Cloud Computing's Environmental Benefits," *Forbes*, June 11, 2013, https://www.forbes.com/sites/uciliawang/2013/06/11/a-google-funded-study-quantifies-cloud-computings-environmental-benefits/?sh=51d6ae6453f6.

10. Adele Beardmore, "Uncovering the Environmental Impact of Cloud Computing," Earth.org, October 12, 2020, https://earth.org/environmental-impact-of-cloud-computing/.

11. Jamie Morgan, "5 Reasons Why the Cloud Is Environmentally Friendly," Mission Cloud Services, https://www.missioncloud.com/blog/5-reasons-why-the-cloud-is-environmentally-friendly.

12. "Ørsted Builds a Greener World with Offshore Wind Power and Digital Technology," Microsoft Transform, https://news.microsoft.com/transform/videos/orsted-greener-world-offshore-wind-digital-technology/.

13. "Ørsted Builds a Greener World."

14. Ørsted, "The World's Most Sustainable Energy Company—Three Years Running," https://us.orsted.com/about-orsted/most-sustainable-energy-company.

15. "The 17 Goals," United Nations, https://sdgs.un.org/goals.

16. Mark Lefko, *Global Sustainability* (New York: Morgan James, 2016).

CHAPTER 15: LEVERAGING TECHNOLOGY TO ENGAGE YOUR CUSTOMERS AND TRANSFORM YOUR BUSINESS

1. "Maersk—Disconnected," The North Alliance, https://www.thenorthalliance.com/our-work/maersk-disconnected/.

2. "Inside the Campaign of the Decade: Aldi's 'Like Brands, Only Cheaper,'" *Marketing Week*, December 18, 2019, https://www.marketingweek.com/inside-ad-campaign-of-the-decade-aldi-like-brands-only-cheaper/.

3. Russell Redman, "Aldi to Expand Presence in New York's Long Island," *Supermarket News*, February 13, 2020, https://www.supermarketnews.com/retail-financial/aldi-expand-presence-new-york-s-long-island.

FINAL THOUGHTS

1. 3M Company, *A Century of Innovation: The 3M Story* (3M Company, Maplewood, MN: 2002), https://multimedia.3m.com/mws/media/171240O/3m-century-of-innovation-book.pdf.

2. "Digital Transformation Is Racing Ahead and No Industry Is Immune," *Harvard Business Review*, July 19, 2017, https://hbr.org/sponsored/2017/07/digital-transformation-is-racing- ahead-and-no-industry-is-immune-2.

3. Mark J. Perry, "Only 52 US Companies Have Been on the Fortune 500 Since 1955, Thanks to the 'Creative Destruction' That Fuels Economic Prosperity," American Enterprise Institute, June 3, 2021, https://www.aei.org/carpe-diem/only-52-us-companies-have-been-on-the-fortune-500-since-1955-thanks-to-the-creative-destruction-that-fuels-economic-prosperity-2/.

ACKNOWLEGMENTS

IT HAS BEEN QUITE AN EXCITING JOURNEY. Years ago, in my first graduate studies program, a professor of mine taught me that after reading each case study, new article, and project assignment to always write down your takeaways. I would like to say thank you, professor!

I come from a culture of adaptability and entrepreneurship. My dad is a huge inspiration on my entrepreneurial journey. I would like to thank my parents, the Rushi family, and Zara, Rahul, Ravi, and Izzy for all those long walks to help me think and reflect. Thanks to friends and coaches Felicia Sims, Jill Khalife, Jennifer Johnson, Niti Sanghrajka, Krutee Shah, Mike Acker, Brain Oulton, Pallavi Chitturi, Scott Pellegrino, Surekha Jituri, Rob Cabello, Johannes Jarl, Peter Glasheen, Julia Doria, Allan Fors, Billy Saleebey, Damjan Gjorgjiev and Samanta Davis, Jon Gornstein, Matt Anestis, Ravi Rajani, Jackie Neilson, John Rossman, Geoff Jackson, Tony Makriniotis, and Michael Flood.

Many friends, colleagues, and peers read early drafts of the book, and I'm grateful for their level of talent and the generosity of the time they gave to me. I'd like to offer my sincere appreciation to several people who gave feedback to make improvements: Chuck Dougherty, whose leadership, advice, and encouragement are admired and appreciated. Professor Ron Pierantozzi for your academic lens on suggestions of flow and diversity thought. Todd Stulgis for fact-checking knowledge on global strategy and in-depth technology experience. A special thanks and admiration to Magnus Penker for providing such an insightful foreword to the book.

BOOK TEAM

Michael Levin, with deep gratitude for your collaboration and your friendship. It has been great sharing these lessons and experiences with you.

Gretchen Jackson, for your guidance during the entire process and for talking me into writing this book. You are a great friend who has given me tremendous support!

I would be remiss to forget Jonathan Merkh and his amazing staff at Forefront Books, especially those with whom I worked closely. The editorial director, Jen Gingerich, was an incisive guide for keeping me on track during the editing process and making all things better. Thanks to Lauren Ward for being a great partner and nothing less than perfect collaboration. Thank you to Justin Batt for your strategic publishing knowledge and creativity and for helping me make new connections. I'm fortunate and delighted to have such a great publishing partner in Forefront Books and Worth Books.

Also, thank you to editor Rick Wolff, copyeditor Andrew Bus, cover designer Bruce Gore, and typesetter Mary Susan

ACKNOWLEDGMENTS

Oleson. Thank you to Billie Brownell for your expert help in proofreading and finalizing the project to completion.

Last but not least, there is a long list of companies that have helped shape my understanding of innovation and their approach to making it more predictable and sustainable. Your efforts and successes have inspired me, and I hope you continue to make innovation a priority in your organizations.

INDEX

273

INDEX

INDEX

INDEX